Bhagavad Gītā

English

GH00660446

Michael Beloved / Madhvācārya dās

Bhagavad Gītā English

Format assistant:
- Marcia K. Beloved

Cover Art
- Praful Kharsani

Front/Back Cover Layout + Lord Shiva Art:
- Sir Paul Castagna

Śrī Śrī Krishna-Arjuna Art:
- Terri Stokes-Pineda

Copyright © 2008 --- Michael Beloved

Correspondence   **Email**

Michael Beloved   axisnexus @gmail.com
3703 Foster Ave
Brooklyn NY 11203
USA

ISBN   9780979391637
LCCN   2008906310

Table of Contents

How to use this book:

Make a casual reading initially.
Make a second reading while pausing and considering verses of interest.
Make a third reading while observing the main themes in the discourse.
Finally, make an indepth study of the entire text.

A note on the diacritical marks and pronounciation:
Names like Krishna and Arjuna are accepted in common English usage. Their English spellings occur in the translation without diacritical marks.
Here are some hints *on how to use the diacritical marks for near-exact pronunciation:*
*Letters with a **dot** under them, should be pronounced while the tongue touches and is released curling slightly at the top of palate.*
*The s sound for **ś** carries an h with it and is said as the **sh** sound in **she**.*
*The s sound for **ṣ** carries an h with it and is said as the **sh** sound in **shun**.*
*The h sound for **ḥ** carries an echoing sound of the vowel before it, such that **oḥ** is actually **oho** and **aḥ** is actually **aha**.*

*In many Sanskrit words the **y** sound is said as an **i** sound, especially when the y sound preceeds an a. For instance, prāṇāyāma should be praa-**nai**-aa-muh, rather than praa-naa-**yaa**-muh.*

*The **a** sound is more like **uh** in English, while the **ā** sound is like the a sound in **far**.*

*The **ṛ** sound is like the **ri** sound in r**idge**.*

*The **ph** sound is never reduced to an f sound as in English. The **p sound** is maintained.*

*Whenever **h** occurs after a consonant, its integrity is maintained as an air forced sound.*

*If the h sound occurs after a vowel and a consonant, one should let the consonant remain with the vowel which preceeds it and allow the h sound to carry with the vowel after it, such that Duryodhana is pronounced with the d consonant allied to the o before it and the h sound manages the a after it. Say Dur-**yod-ha**-na or Dur-**yod-han**. Do not say Dur-yo-**dha**-na. Separate the d and h sounds to make them distinct. In words where you have no choice and must combine the d and h sound, as in the word dharma. Make sure that the **h sound** is heard as an **air sound pushed out from the throat**. Dharma should never be mistaken for darma. But adharma should be **ad-har-**ma.*

*The **c** sound is **ch,** and the **ch** sound is **ch-h**.*

Introduction

This translation, using the Bhagavad-Gītā as well as the Mahābhārata from which the text was extracted, gives a view of the cultural and social conditions in which Arjuna queried and Sri Krishna answered. This was motivated by a desire to show that Sri Krishna's ideas were mostly centered on yoga practice as it could be applied to cultural life. That is karma yoga, which is karma and yoga, or cultural activities and the practice of meditative yoga.

Readers should always keep in mind that this discourse took place under military conditions and not under a religious ceremonial atmosphere. Today the Bhagavad-Gītā is used mostly in temples and it is considered a religious text, but it was delivered to a battle commander on a warfield. This is an easy-read translation which renders the deep insights of Sri Krishna in plain modern English. Bhagavad-Gītā is a rare text, a special gift to humanity. It maps the inside of the human psyche and discusses the influences and range of matter, spirit and the Supreme Spirit.

Relax yourself! Read on!

CHAPTER 1

Arjuna's Discouragement*

Dhṛtarāṣṭra said: O Sanjaya, being possessed with battle spirit and meeting together, what did my sons and the sons of Pandu do at Kurukṣetra, the place for settling political affairs? (1.1)

Sanjaya said: Indeed, after observing the Pandava army which was set in a battle formation, the Crown Prince Duryodhana, while approaching the Military Teacher, said this remark: (1.2)

Sir, see this great army of the sons of Pandu, which is set for combat by your perceptive student, the son of Drupada. (1.3)

Here are heroes, great bowmen, who are equal in battle to Bhima and Arjuna. There is Yuyudhāna, Virāṭa, and Drupada, the great chariot fighter. (1.4)

There is Dhṛṣṭaketu, Cekitāna, and the Kāśi ruler, that valiant man. There is Purujit and Kuntibhoja and Śaibya, the bull-bodied man. (1.5)

There is the valiant Yudhāmanyu and the heroic Uttamauja. There are the son of Subhadrā and the sons of Draupadī, who indeed, are all champions of chariot warfare. (1.6)

---

*The Mahābhārata contains no chapter headings. This title was assigned by the translator on the basis of verse 27 of this chapter.

But, O best of the initiates, be informed of our men who are distinguished. For the sake of giving information to you, I mention the leaders of my army. (1.7)

There is your qualified self, and Bhishma, Karṇa and Kṛpa who are victorious in battle. There is also Aśvatthāma, Vikarṇa and the son of Somadatta. (1.8)

And many other heroes wielding various weapons, being experts in warfare, would give their lives for my sake. (1.9)

Inadequate is this military force of ours which is supervised by Bhishma. Sufficient, however, is their military power which is protected by Bhīma. (1.10)

And in all maneuvers, as positioned by assignment, all you honorable masters should definitely protect Bhishma. (1.11)

The eldest Kuru, the grandfather, voluminously blew his conchshell, sounding a loud lion-like roar, thus producing great happiness for Duryodhana. (1.12)

And then the conches and kettledrums, the cymbals, drums and trumpets, were simultaneously sounded. That sound was tumultuous. (1.13)

Then, standing in a magnificent, swift-moving chariot with white horses harnessed, the descendant of Madhu and the son of Pandu blew two supernatural conchshells. (1.14)

The conchshell named Pāñcajanya was blown by Hṛṣīkeśa, Krishna. The Devadatta conch was sounded by the conqueror of wealthy countries, Arjuna. Bhīma, the wolf-bellied man whose actions are terrible, blew the great conch named Paundra. (1.15)

The King, Kuntī's son, Yudhishthira, blew the Anantavijayam. Nakula and Sahadeva blew the Sughosha and Manipushpaka respectively. (1.16)

The King of Kāśi, the superior bowman, and Śikhandī, the great chariot fighter, Dhṛṣṭadyumna and Virata and Sātyaki, the unconquered one, (1.17)

...O king of the province, Drupada and the sons of Draupadī, being grouped together, and the strong-armed son of Subhadrā, blew conchshells in series. (1.18)

The noise disrupted the emotions of the sons of Dhṛtarāṣṭra, and the vibrating sound caused the sky and earth to resonate. (1.19)

Then after observing the sons of Dhṛtarāṣṭra in battle formation, the man with a monkey insignia, that son of Pandu, raised his bow in the challenge of the clash of weapons. (1.20)

Then he spoke this request to Hṛṣīkeśa, Krishna: O Lord of the earth, cause my chariot to be parked in the midst of the two armies, O unaffected one, (1.21)

...so that I can see these battle-hungry, armed warriors, with whom I should fight in this battle engagement. (1.22)

I wish to observe those who are to fight, who assembled here desiring to please the evil-minded son of King Dhṛtarāṣṭra, in battle. (1.23)

Sanjaya said: O descendant of Bharata, thus being addressed by Arjuna, the thick-haired baron, Krishna, who is known as Hṛṣīkeśa, caused the best of the chariots to be positioned in the midst of the two armies. (1.24)

In the presence of Bhishma, Droṇa and all those rulers of the earth, Krishna said: O son of Pṛthā, behold these Kurus who are assembled here together. (1.25)

The son of Pṛthā saw men who were fathers, grandfathers, revered teachers, maternal uncles, brothers, sons, grandsons, as well as friends, fathers-in-law and well-wishing friends, standing there in both armies. (1.26)

Observing all his relatives in the armored state, that son of Kuntī was overwhelmed by deep compassion. Feeling discouraged, he spoke this: (1.27)

Having seen this situation of my own people, standing near, eager for combat, my legs collapse and my mouth dries up. (1.28)

A trembling is in my body and a bristling of my hairs takes place. The Gāṇḍīva bow falls from my hand. Indeed, my skin burns. (1.29)

I cannot remain standing. My mind feels as if it wavers. I perceive bad indications, O beautiful-haired one. (1.30)

And I can imagine no benefit in killing off my kinfolk in battle. I do not desire victory, O Krishna, or political power, or good feelings. (1.31)

What value to us would there be with political control of a nation, O Chief of the cowherds? What use would there be with the enjoyable aspects or with life? Those in whose interest, the political control, the enjoyments and pleasures, were desired by us, (1.32)

...(they) are armed in battle formation, having left aside their lives and financial assets. These are revered teachers, fathers, sons and also grandfathers, (1.33)

...brothers of our mothers, fathers of our wives, grandsons, brothers-in-law, and also their relatives. O slayer of Madhu, I do not desire to slay them even though they are intent on killing, (1.34)

...even for political control of the three sectors of the universe, how then for the earth? O motivator of people, what joy should be had by killing the sons of Dhṛtarāṣṭra? (1.35)

Having killed the offenders, sin will take hold of us. Therefore we are not justified to kill the sons of Dhṛtarāṣṭra, our relatives. Having killed our own people, how should we be happy, O descendant of Madhu? (1.36)

Even if these persons, their minds being possessed by greed, do not see the fault caused by the destruction of the clan and the crime of hurting a friend, (1.37)

...O motivator of human beings, why, by due reason, should we not understand that we should turn away from this sin, the crime caused by the destruction of the clan? (1.38)

In the destruction of the clan, the ancient family traditions vanish. In the removal of the traditional values, the entire clan is overpowered by lawlessness. (1.39)

Due to the predominance of lawlessness, the women of the clan are degraded. In such women, O clansman of the Vṛṣṇis, there arises the sexual intermixture of the classes. (1.40)

Indeed, the sexual intermixture causes the destroyers of the clan and the clan itself to go to hell. The departed ancestors of those clansmen, being deprived of the psychic cakes and water which are offered ceremonially, are degraded. (1.41)

By the sins of the family destroyers and by the sexual intermixture of the classes, individual skills and traditional family duties disappear. (1.42)

O Krishna, those who destroy the family customs dwell in hell indefinitely. This was declared repeatedly. (1.43)

O! What a wonder! We are committed to perform a great sin, being eager to kill our kinfolk, through greed for aristocratic pleasures. (1.44)

If the weapon-bearing sons of Dhṛtarāṣṭra should kill me in battle, while I was unresisting, and unarmed, this to me would be greater pleasure. (1.45)

Having spoken, Arjuna, who was in the midst of the conflict, sat down on his chariot. Casting aside his arrow and bow, he was overwhelmed with sorrow. (1.46)

CHAPTER 2

The Divine State*

Sanjaya said: To him who was overcome with pity, whose eyes were filled with tears, who was perplexed and saddened with hopelessness, the killer of Madhu spoke this response: (2.1)

The Blessed Lord said: How has this sickly emotion come to you at a crucial time? It is not suitable for a cultured man. It does not facilitate heaven in the hereafter. It causes disgrace, O Arjuna. (2.2)

O son of Pṛthā, you should not entertain cowardly behavior. This is not suitable for you. Give up this degrading emotional weakness. Stand, O scorcher of the enemy. (2.3)

Arjuna said: How will I attack in battle, Bhishma and Droṇa, who are worthy of reverence, O Krishna? (2.4)

In fact, it is better to eat by begging in this world than by killing the revered teachers who are great-natured. But having slain the venerable teachers on the basis of impulsive desires, I would enjoy blood-stained luxuries here on earth. (2.5)

The Mahābhārata contains no chapter headings. This title was assigned by the translator on the basis of verse 72 of this chapter.

And this we do not know, which of the alternatives is better; whether we should conquer or if they should triumph over us. It concerns these sons of Dhṛtarāṣṭra who stand armed before us, and whom we would not desire to outlive, if they are killed. (2.6)

As a mercy-prone man, overcome by these feelings of pity, with my sense of duty clouded by mental confusion, I ask You to tell me with certainty, what is preferable. I am a student of Yours. Instruct me, who am submitted to You. (2.7)

In fact, I do not see, what would remove the sadness that absorbs my enthusiasm, even unrivaled rulership and prosperity on earth or sovereignty over the angelic kingdom. (2.8)

Sanjaya said: O Dhṛtarāṣṭra, scorcher of enemies, after appealing to Krishna, Arjuna said to Govinda, the chief of cowherds, "I will not fight." Having said this, he became silent. (2.9)

Then, in the middle of both armies, Krishna, who was smiling, spoke this speech to the dejected Arjuna. (2.10)

The Blessed Lord said: You mourned for that which should not be regretted. And you expressed intelligent statements. Educated persons mourn neither for those who are embodied or departed.(2.11)

There was never a time when I did not exist, nor you nor these rulers of the people. Nor will we cease to exist from now onwards. (2.12)

As the embodied soul endures childhood, youth and old age, so another body is acquired in sequence. The wise person is not confused on this topic. (2.13)

O son of Kuntī, mundane sensations which cause cold and heat, pleasure and pain, do come and go. Cope with them, O man of the Bharata family. (2.14)

O bull among men, these mundane sensations do not afflict the wise man who is steady in miserable or enjoyable conditions. That person is fit for immortality. (2.15)

Of the non-substantial things, there is no enduring existence. Of the substantial things, there is no lack of existence. These two truths were perceived with certainty by the mystic seers of reality. (2.16)

Know that indestructible factor by which all this world is pervaded. No one can accomplish the destruction of that everlasting principle. (2.17)

It is declared that the bodies of the eternal, indestructible and immeasurable embodied soul are terminal. Therefore fight, descendant of the Bharatas. (2.18)

Both viewers do not understand, namely: He who concludes that the embodied soul is the killer and he who thinks that the embodied soul is killed. The embodied soul does not kill nor can he be killed. (2.19)

This embodied soul is not born, nor does it die at any time, nor having existed will it not be. Being birthless, eternal, perpetual and primeval, it is not slain in the act of killing the body. (2.20)

O son of Pṛthā, how can the person who knows this indestructible, eternal, birthless and imperishable principle, cause someone to be killed or even kill someone directly? (2.21)

As when discarding old clothing, a person takes new garments, so the embodied soul abandons old bodies taking new ones. (2.22)

Weapons do not pierce, fire does not burn, and water does not wet, nor does the wind dry that embodied soul. (2.23)

This embodied soul cannot be pierced, cannot be burnt, cannot be moistened, and cannot be dried. And indeed, this soul is eternal. It can penetrate all things. It is a permanent principle and is stable and primeval. (2.24)

This embodied soul is undisplayed, unimaginable, and unchanging. Therefore knowing this, you should not lament. (2.25)

And furthermore if you think that this embodied soul is continually being born or continually dying, even so, O strong-armed man, you should not lament. (2.26)

In fact, of that which is born, death is certain; of that which is dead, birth is certain. Therefore in assessing what is unavoidable, you should not lament. (2.27)

The living beings are undetected in the beginning of a manifestation, visible in the interim stages, and are again undetected at the end of a manifestation. What is the complaint?(2.28)

Someone perceives this embodied soul as being wonderful. Another person describes it as amazing. Another hears of it as being fantastic. And even after hearing this, no one knows this embodied soul in fact. (2.29)

In the body, in all cases, this embodied soul is always non-killable, O descendant of Bharata. Therefore you should not mourn for any of these beings. (2.30)

And considering your assigned duty, you should not look for alternatives. In fact, for the son of a king, there is no other duty which is better than a righteous battle. (2.31)

And by a stroke of luck, the gate of heaven is opened. Thrilled are the warriors who get such a battle opportunity, O son of Pṛthā. (2.32)

Now if you do not conduct this righteous war, then, by neglecting your duty and reputation, you will acquire a fault. (2.33)

The people will speak of your downfall continually. And for an honored man, the loss of reputation is harder to bear than the loss of his body. (2.34)

The great warriors will think that because of fear, you withdrew from battle. And to those who held a big opinion, you will appear to be insignificant. (2.35)

The enemies will say many slurs about you, thus laughing at your capability. But, what would be a greater grief than this?   (2.36)

Either be killed and achieve the angelic world or having conquered, enjoy the nation. Therefore stand up and be decisive, O son of Kuntī. (2.37)

Having regarded happiness, distress, gains, losses, victory and defeat, as the same emotions, apply yourself to battle. Thus you will get no demerit. (2.38)

As explained in the Sāṁkhya philosophy, this vision is the insight, but hear of its application in yoga practice. Yoked with this insight, O son of Pṛthā, you will avoid the complication of action. (2.39)

In this insight, no endeavor is lost nor is there any reversal. Even a little of this righteous practice protects from the great danger. (2.40)

When a person's intentional determination is guided by technical insight, he experiences one view, O dear man of the Kuru family. But the views of a person with many hopes are diverse and endless. (2.41)

This is poetic quotation which the ignorant reciters proclaim, O son of Pṛthā. Enjoying the Vedic verses, they say there is no other written authority. (2.42)

Those reciters, being people of a sensuous nature, being intent on going to the Svarga angelic world, offering such rebirth as payoff for cultural activities, make themselves busy in various specific ceremonial rites, and focusing on enjoyment and political power. (2.43)

Being absorbed by this way of life, pleasure-prone and power-seeking people, are captivated by this idea. Thus in meditation, the self-focused intellect is not experienced by them. (2.44)

Three moody phases are offered by the Vedas. Be without the three moods, O Arjuna. Be without the moody fluctuations. Be always anchored to reality. Be free from grasping and possessiveness. (2.45)

For as much importance as there is in a well when suitable water flows in all directions, so much worth is in the entire Vedas for a perceptive brahmin. (2.46)

The command is yours while performing, but not at any time in the aftermath of consequences. Do not be motivated by a result, nor harbor an attachment to idleness. (2.47)

So perform actions in the yoga mood. Attachment to crippling emotions should be abandoned, O conqueror of wealthy countries. Be indifferent to success or failure. It is said that indifference denotes yoga. (2.48)

Surely, cultural action is by far inferior to intellectual discipline through yoga, O victor of wealthy countries. One should take shelter in mystic insight for how pathetic are those who are motivated by the promise of results. (2.49)

A person who is disciplined by the reality-piercing insight disregards in each life both pleasant and unpleasant work. Therefore take to the yogic mood. Yoga gives skill in performance. (2.50)

Having abandoned the results which are produced by actions, and being freed from the bondage of rebirth, those wise people, the disciplined mystic seers, go to the misery-free place. (2.51)

When from your delusion-saturated mind, your discrimination departs, you will become disgusted with what is to be heard and what was heard. (2.52)

When, rejecting misleading scriptural information, your intelligence remains steady without moody variation, being situated in deep meditation, you will master the yoga disciplines. (2.53)

Arjuna said: In regards to the person who is situated in clear, penetrating insight, would you please describe him? Speak of the person who is anchored in deep meditation, O Keśava Krishna. As for the man who is steady in objectives, how would he speak? How would he sit? How would he act? (2.54)

The Blessed Lord said: When someone abandons all cravings, O son of Pṛthā, and escapes from mental dominance, being self content, then that person is identified as one with steady insight. (2.55)

Furthermore, someone who in miserable conditions remains free from worries, and who in good conditions remains free from excitement, who steps aside from passion, fear and anger, and who is steady in meditation is considered to be a wise man. (2.56)

A person who, in all circumstances, is without crippling affections, who, when meeting enjoyable or disturbing factors, does not get excited nor distressed, his reality-piercing consciousness is established. (2.57)

When such a person pulls fully out of moods, he or she may be compared to the tortoise with its limbs retracted. The senses are withdrawn from the attractive things in the case of a person whose reality-piercing vision is established. (2.58)

The temptations themselves turn away from the disciplinary attitude of an ascetic, but the memory of previous indulgences remain with him. When he experiences higher stages, those memories leave him. (2.59)

Concerning an aspiring seeker, O son of Kuntī, concerning a discerned educated person, the senses do torment him. By impulses the senses do adjust his mentality. (2.60)

Restraining all these senses, being disciplined in yoga practice, an ascetic should sit, being focused on Me. The vision of a person whose sensuality is controlled, remains anchored in reality. (2.61)

The act of considering sensual objects, creates in a person, an attachment to them. From attachment comes craving. From this craving, anger is derived. (2.62)

From anger, comes delusion. From this delusion, the conscience vanishes. When he loses judgment, his discerning power fades away. Once the discernment is affected, he is ruined. (2.63)

If, on the other hand, cravings and dislikings are continued and the attractive objects and senses continue interaction, a disciplined person who is usually well-behaved, gets the grace of providence. (2.64)

By the grace of providence, all the emotional distresses cease for him. Being of a pacified mind, his intelligence at once, becomes stable. (2.65)

In comparison, never is there proper discernment in an uncontrolled person. He is not capable of concentration. One who lacks concentration cannot get inner peace. For one who lacks emotional stability, how will happiness be achieved? (2.66)

When the mind is prompted by the wandering senses, it utilizes the discernment, just as in water, the wind handles a ship. (2.67)

Thus, O Arjuna, concerning the person who, in every interaction retracts the sensual feelings from the attractive objects; his discernment remains constant. (2.68)

The sense-controlling person is perceptive of that which is void to the ordinary people. What is exciting to the masses of people is void to the perceptive sage. (2.69)

Becoming filled, not flowing about, remaining stationary, the ocean absorbs the waters that enter it. Similarly, a person who remains calm when cravings arise gets true satisfaction, but not the person who craves for every desire. (2.70)

The person who rejects all cravings, whose acts are free of lusty motivation, who is indifferent to possessions, who is free of impulsive assertion, attains contentment. (2.71)

This divine state is required, O son of Pṛthā. If a man does not have this, he is stupefied. At the time of death, the full stoppage of mundane sensuality and the attainment of divinity is attained by one who is fixed in this divine state. (2.72)

CHAPTER 3

Cultural Activity and

Renunciation*

Arjuna contested: O motivator of men, if it is Your idea that the mental approach is better than the physically-active one, then why do You urge me to commit horrible action, O handsome-haired One? (3.1)

You baffle my intelligence with this two-way proposal. Mention one priority, by which I would surely get the best result. (3.2)

The Blessed Lord said: In the physical world, a two-fold standard was previously taught by Me, O Arjuna, my good man. This was mind regulation by the yoga practice of the Sāṁkhya philosophical yogis and the action regulation by the yoga practice of the non-philosophical yogis. (3.3)

A man does not attain freedom from cultural activity merely by not being involved in social affairs. And not by renunciation alone, does he achieve spiritual perfection. (3.4)

*The Mahābhārata contains no chapter headings. This title was assigned by the translator on the basis of verse 4 of this chapter.

No one, even momentarily, ever exists without vibration. By the variations of mundane energy in material nature, everyone, even against their wishes, is forced to perform. (3.5)

A person who, while restraining his bodily limbs, sits with the mind, remembering attractive objects, is a deceiver. So it is declared. (3.6)

However, whosoever endeavors to control the senses by the mind, O Arjuna, and who restricts the limbs through regulating his work by yoga practice, without attachment, is superior. (3.7)

Moral action should be done by you. Performance is better than non-performance. Even the maintenance of your body could not be achieved without activity. (3.8)

Besides action for religious fulfillment and ceremony, this world is action-bound. Act for the sake of religious fulfillment and ceremony, O son of Kuntī. Be free from attachment. Act promptly. (3.9)

Long ago, having created the first human beings, along with religious fulfillment and ceremonies, the Procreator Brahmā said: By this worship procedure, you may be productive. May it cause the fulfillment of your desires. (3.10)

By this procedure, you may cause the supernatural rulers to flourish. They, in turn, may bless you. In favorably regarding each other, the highest well-being will be achieved. (3.11)

The supernatural rulers, being manifested through prescribed austerity and religious ceremony, will, indeed, give you the most desired people and things. Whosoever does not offer those given items to them, but who enjoys these, is certainly a thief. (3.12)

(Krishna continued): The virtuous people who utilize the items after they are sanctified by prescribed ceremony, are released from all faults. But the wicked ones who prepare for their own sake, consume their own impurity. (3.13)

The creatures are produced from nourishment. From rain clouds, nourishment originated. From prescribed austerity and religious ceremony, rain clouds are produced. And prescribed austerity and religious ceremony are caused by cultural activities. (3.14)

Cultural activity is produced from the Personified Veda. The Personified Veda comes from the unaffected Supreme Spirit. Hence the all-pervading Supreme Spirit is always situated in prescribed austerity and religious ceremony. (3.15)

O son of Pṛthā, a person who does not cause this circular process to be perpetuated here on earth, lives as a malicious, sensually-happy and worthless person. (3.16)

A person who is spiritually-pleased, self-satisfied and internally-content, has no cultural duties. (3.17)

The person who does not aspire for gain in an action or in an inaction, is not reliant on any mundane creature. (3.18)

Therefore, being always unattached, perform the action which is your duty. By being detached and executing the required tasks, a person gets the highest stage. (3.19)

Beginning with Janaka, perfection was attained by cultural activities alone. Seeing the necessity for world maintenance, you should act. (3.20)

Whatever a great person does, for that only, others aspire. Whatever trend he establishes, the world pursues. (3.21)

For Me, O son of Pṛthā, there is nothing specific that must be done in the three divisions of the universe. And there is nothing that I have not attained nor should acquire, and yet I function in cultural activities. (3.22)

If perchance, I did not perform attentively, then all human beings, O son of Pṛthā, would follow Me in all respects. (3.23)

If I should not engage in cultural activity, these worlds would perish. And I would be a producer of social chaos. I would have destroyed these creatures. (3.24)

As the unintelligent people perform with attachment to cultural activity, O son of the Bharata family, so the wise person should act, but in a detached manner, for the maintenance of society. (3.25)

One should not produce indetermination in the minds of the simpletons. A wise person should inspire them to be satisfied by action. The wise one should be disciplined in behavior. (3.26)

In all cases, actions are performed by variations of the primal mundane energy. But the identity-confused person thinks: "I am the performer." (3.27)

But, O powerful man, having considered that variations of material nature interact with variations of material nature, the reality-perceiving person is not attached to action. (3.28)

Those who are deluded by the variations of material nature are attached to mood-motivated activities. The person who understands the reality should not unsettle those foolish people who have partial insight. (3.29)

All your working power should be entrusted to Me. On the Supreme Spirit, you should meditate. Being free from cravings, indifferent to selfishness, do fight. Be a man whose feverish mood has departed. (3.30)

Those human beings, who believe My idea, constantly applying it, having faith, not complaining, are freed from the consequences of action. (3.31)

Know that those who discredit this instruction and do not practice My ideas, being of muddled insight, are jinxed and senseless. (3.32)

A human being, even a wise man, acts according to his material nature. The creatures submit to material nature. What will restraint do? (3.33)

The response of liking or disliking that is felt between a sense and an attractive object, is deep-seated. One should not be influenced by the power of these two moods. They are hindrances. (3.34)

Better to do one's righteous duty imperfectly, than to do the duty of another with great efficiency. Death is better in the course of one's duty but the task of another is risky. (3.35)

Arjuna said: Then explain, O family man of the Vṛṣṇis, by what is a person forced to commit an evil unwillingly, just as if he were compelled to do so? (3.36)

The Blessed Lord said: This force is craving. This power is anger. The passionate emotion is the source. It has a great consuming power and does much damage. Recognize it as the enemy in this case. (3.37)

As the sacrificial fire is obscured by smoke, and similarly as a mirror is shrouded by dust or as an embryo is covered by skin, so a man's insight is blocked by the passionate energy. (3.38)

The discernment of educated people is adjusted by their eternal enemy which is the sense of yearning for various things. O son of Kuntī, the lusty power, is as hard to satisfy as it is to keep a fire burning. (3.39)

It is authoritatively stated that the senses, the mind and the intelligence are the combined warehouse of the passionate enemy. By these faculties, the lusty power confuses the embodied soul, shrouding his insight. (3.40)

Thus regulating the senses initially, you should, O powerful man of the Bharata family, squelch this degrading power which ruins knowledge and discernment. (3.41)

The ancient psychologists say that the senses are energetic, but in comparison to the senses, the mind is more energetic. In contrast to the mind, the intelligence is even more sensitive. But in reference, the spirit is most elevated. (3.42)

Thus having understood what is higher than intelligence, keeping the personal energies under control of the spirit, uproot, O powerful man, the enemy, the form of passionate desire which is difficult to grasp. (3.43)

CHAPTER 4

Disciplines of

Accomplishment*

The Blessed Lord said: I explained to Vivasvat, this perpetual teaching of controlling the personal energies through yoga. Vivasvat explained it to Manu. Manu imparted it to Ikṣvāku. (4.1)

Thus, received through a series of teachers, the yogi kings knew this skill of controlling the personal energies. After a long time, here on earth, this yoga application was lost, O burner of enemy forces. (4.2)

Today, this ancient yoga technique is explained to you by Me, since you are devoted to Me and are My friend. Indeed, this is confidential and is the best teaching. (4.3)

Arjuna said: Your Lordship's birth was later. The birth of Vivasvat was earlier. How should I understand that You explained this before? (4.4)

The Blessed Lord said: Many of My births transpired, and yours, Arjuna. I recall them all. You do not remember, O scorcher of the enemies. (4.5)

*The Mahābhārata contains no chapter headings. This title was assigned by the translator on the basis of verse 32 of this chapter.

Even though I am birthless and My person is imperishable, and even though I am the Lord of the creatures, by controlling My material energies, I become visible by My supernatural power. (4.6)

Whenever there is a decrease of righteousness, O son of the Bharata family, and when there is an increase of wickedness, then I show Myself. (4.7)

To protect the saintly people, to destroy the wicked ones, and to establish righteousness, I come into the visible existence from era to era. (4.8)

One who knows My supernatural visitation and deeds, who truly realizes this while abandoning his body, does not seek rebirth. He goes to Me, O Arjuna. (4.9)

Many whose craving, fear and anger are gone, who are totally focused on Me, who are purified by austerity and education, attained My level of existence. (4.10)

As they rely on Me, so I relate to them, O son of Pṛthā. All human beings, everywhere, are affected by My course of action. (4.11)

Wanting their ritual action to succeed, people in the world, worship the supernatural authorities. Quickly in this human world, there is fulfillment which comes from ritual action. (4.12)

According to the distribution of habits and work tendencies, the four career categories were instituted by Me. Know that I am never required to participate. (4.13)

Actions do not entrap Me. The desire for payoff is not in Me. The person who understands this is not entrapped by action. (4.14)

Having understood this conclusion, functional work was done, even by the yogi kings who desired liberation. Therefore you should perform cultural acts, just as it was done before. (4.15)

What is action? What is not an action? Even eloquent philosophers are confused on this subject. I will discuss the subject of action with you. Knowing this, you will be freed from undesirable circumstances. (4.16)

Indeed, appropriate action should be known and one should also recognize the inappropriate type. The effect of no action should be understood. The course of action is difficult to comprehend. (4.17)

He who perceives the non-acting factor in a performance and sees an acting factor when there is no action, is the wise person among human beings. He is skilled in yoga and can perform all actions. (4.18)

He for whom desire and intention are not mixed into his endeavors, who has destroyed reactionary work by the fiery force of his knowledge, he, the wise men call a pandit or learned man. (4.19)

Giving up the quest for a payoff from actions, being always satisfied, not depending on anything, he does nothing at all even while performing. (4.20)

Without hoping, being reserved in thought and spirit, giving up all tendency for grasping, using the body effectively for action, he does not acquire a fault. (4.21)

Being satisfied by benefit which comes by chance, ignoring likes and dislikes, being free from envy, even-minded in success and failure, and having performed, a man is still not implicated. (4.22)

Concerning a person whose attachment is finished, who is liberated, whose idea is established in knowledge, any of his action which is done solely for austerity and religion, does cancel completely. (4.23)

Spiritual existence is the basis of his ceremonial articles. It is the foundation of sacrificial ingredients. The perceptive priest pours the stipulated items into the fiery splendor of spiritual existence. It is the spiritual existence which is attained by a person who keeps contact with the spiritual level while acting. (4.24)

Some yogis perform austerity and religious ceremony in relation to a supernatural authority. Others offer austerity and religious ceremony as the sacrifice into the fiery brilliance of spiritual existence. (4.25)

Other yogis offer hearing and other sensual powers into the fiery power of restraint. Some offer sound and other sensual pursuits into the fiery sensual power. (4.26)

Some ascetics subject the sensual actions and the breath function to self-restraint by fiery yoga austerities, which are illuminated by experience. (4.27)

Persons whose austerity and religious ceremony involve the control of material possession, those whose austerity and religious life involve some self-denial, as well as some others whose penance and religious procedure is the eight-part yoga discipline, and those whose austerity and religious ceremony is the study of the Veda and the acquirement of knowledge, all these are regarded as ascetics with strict vows. (4.28)

Some offer inhalation into the exhalation channels; similarly others offer the exhalation into the inhalation channels, thus being determined to regulate the channels of the energizing and de-energizing airs. (4.29)

Others who were restrained in diet, impel fresh air into the previously inhaled air. All these ascetics whose impurities were removed by austerity and religious ceremony understand the value of an act of sacrifice. (4.30)

Those who enjoy the physical and psychological results of a sacrifice, go to the primeval spiritual region. This world is not properly utilized by those who do not perform austerity or religious ceremony. How then can the other world be, O best of the Kurus? (4.31)

Many types of disciplines of accomplishment were expounded in the mouth of the spiritual existence. Know them all to be produced from action. Realizing this, O Arjuna, you will be freed. (4.32)

Better than property control and its ritual regulation is knowledge control and its ritual regulation, O scorcher of the enemy. Every activity without exception, O son of Pṛthā, is realized as a conclusion in the final analysis. (4.33)

This you ought to know. By submitting yourself as a student, by asking questions and by serving as requested, the perceptive reality-conversant teachers will teach you the knowledge. (4.34)

Having known that experience, you will never again succumb to delusion, O son of Pandu. By that experience, you will perceive all beings in relation to yourself and then in relation to Me. (4.35)

Even if you were the most wicked of the culprits, you will overcome all bad tendencies by the conveyance of this experience. (4.36)

As when wood is set on fire, it is reduced to ashes, O Arjuna, so the fiery potency of realized knowledge reduces all actions to nothing. (4.37)

Nothing, indeed, can be compared with direct experience. No other purifier is as relevant in this world. That man who himself is perfected in yoga practice, will in time, locate the realization in himself. (4.38)

One who has faith, gets the experience. Being devoted to restraining the sensual energy, having acquired the experience, he goes quickly to the supreme peace. (4.39)

The ignorant person, the faithless one who is doubtful, is degraded. Neither this physical world, nor the dimensions beyond this, nor happiness, is for the person who is doubtful. (4.40)

Cultural activities do not implicate a person whose actions are renounced through techniques developed in yoga practice, whose doubt is removed by realized knowledge and who is self-composed, O conqueror of wealthy countries. (4.41)

Therefore having severed entirely with the cutting instrument of realized knowledge, this doubt that comes from the ignorance lodged in your being, resort to yogic technique and make a stand, O man of the Bharata family! (4.42)

CHAPTER 5

Disciplined Use of

Opportunities

by a Yogi*

Arjuna said: You approved renunciation of social activity and also mentioned the application of yoga to worldly life. Which one of these is better? Tell me this with certainty. (5.1)

The Blessed Lord said: Both methods, the total renunciation of social opportunities and the disciplined use of opportunities by a yogi, lead to ultimate happiness. But of the two aspects, the disciplined use of opportunities in a yogic mood is better than total renunciation of cultural activity. (5.2)

Indeed, a person who neither dislikes nor craves, who is indifferent to opposite features, should be recognized as a consistent renouncer, O strong-armed man. He is easily freed from implication. (5.3)

*The Mahābhārata contains no chapter headings. This title was assigned by the translator on the basis of verse 2 of this chapter.

It is the simple-minded people, not the perceptive speakers, who say that Sāṁkhya ideas and yoga practices are separate. Even if one method is practised correctly, the practitioner gets the result of either. (5.4)

The level obtained by the Sāṁkhya experts is also reached by the yogis. Sāṁkhya and yoga are essentially one. He who perceives that really sees. (5.5)

Renunciation of opportunities is difficult to attain without yoga practice, O mighty man. In the nick of time, a yoga-proficient sage reaches the spiritual plane. (5.6)

A person who is proficient in yoga, whose soul is purified, who is self-controlled, who has conquered his senses, whose self feels related to all beings, is not implicated when acting. (5.7)

"I do not initiate anything." Being proficient in yoga, this is what the knower of reality thinks. While seeing, hearing, touching, smelling, eating, walking, sleeping and breathing, (5.8)

...while talking, evacuating, holding, opening and closing the eyelids, he considers, "The senses are interlocked with the attractive objects." (5.9)

Being focused on the spiritual level, discarding attachments, his acts are not defiled by necessary violence, just as a lotus leaf is not affected by water. (5.10)

With the body, mind and intelligence, or even with the senses alone, the yogis, having discarded attachment, perform cultural acts for self-purification. (5.11)

The person who is proficient in yoga, and who abandons the rewards of cultural activity, obtains steady peace. The person who is not proficient in yoga, being attached to results, is bound by desire-motivated action. (5.12)

Renouncing all action with the mind, the embodied soul resides happily within as the director in the nine-gated city, not acting nor causing activity. (5.13)

The Lord does not create the means of action, nor the actions of the creatures, nor the action-consequence cycle. But the inherent nature causes this. (5.14)

The Almighty God does not receive from anyone, an evil consequence nor a good reaction. The knowledge of this is shrouded by ignorance through which the people are deluded. (5.15)

However, for those, in whose souls the ignorance is removed by experience, that revelation of theirs, will cause the Supreme Truth to appear distinctly like the sun. (5.16)

Those whose intellects are situated in that Supreme Truth, whose souls are focused on it, whose basic reference is that, whose faults are removed by the experience, who aspire to that as the highest reality, never go again to rebirth. (5.17)

In a learned, trained, accomplished brahmin, in a cow, an elephant, a dog, or a dog-flesh eater, the scripturally-conversant mystic seers observe a common factor. (5.18)

Here in this world, birth is conquered by those whose minds are established in impartiality. Indeed, pure spirit is faultless and equally disposed. Therefore they are established on the pure spiritual plane. (5.19)

Having attained a desired item or favorable circumstance, a person should not become excited. Having attained something unpleasant, he should not detest it. With stable intelligence, without confusion, a person who continually experiences the spiritual reality, remains situated on the spiritual plane. (5.20)

The person who is not attached to the external sensations, who finds happiness in the spirit, whose spirit is linked to the spiritual plane through yoga process, makes contact with the non-fluctuating happiness. (5.21)

The pleasures that come from sensual contacts are sources of pain. They have a beginning and ending, O son of Kuntī. A wise person never delights in them. (5.22)

The person who, before leaving the body, endures the craving-based, anger-based impulsions, is disciplined. He is a happy human being. (5.23)

The person who is happy within, who is spiritually delighted and as a result, experiences the brilliant consciousness, he, that yogi, experiences the stoppage of disturbing sensuality and attains constant spirituality in absorption on the spiritual plane. (5.24)

Those seers whose sins and faults are terminated, whose doubts are removed, whose souls are restrained, who find joy in regarding the welfare of the creatures, attain a cessation of their material existence and a simultaneous absorption in spirituality. (5.25)

The cessation of material existence and assumption of enlightened spirituality is soon to be attained by those ascetics whose thinking is restrained and who understand the spiritual self. (5.26)

Excluding the external sensual contacts, and fixing the visual focus between the eyebrows, putting the inhalation and exhalation in balance, moving through the nose... (5.27)

...the wise man, who is dedicated to achieving liberation, whose sensual energy, mind and intellect are controlled, whose desire, fear and anger are gone, is liberated always. (5.28)

Recognizing Me, as the enjoyer of religious ceremonies and austerities, the Supreme God of the entire world, the friend of the creatures, he attains spiritual peace. (5.29)

CHAPTER 6

Yoga Practice*

The Blessed Lord said: A person who fulfills obligatory action, without depending on the result of the action, is a renouncer, and a yogi, not the one who is without a fire ceremony or who lacks physical activity. (6.1)

That which the authorities define as renunciation, know it as applied yoga, O Arjuna Pandava. Indeed, no one becomes a yogi without an intention for renunciation. (6.2)

For a philosophical man who strives for yoga expertise, cultural activity is recommended. For one who has mastered yoga already, the tranquil reserved method is the means. (6.3)

Indeed, when having discarded all motivations, a person feels no attachment to attractive objects nor to performance, he is said to be proficient in yoga practice. (6.4)

One should elevate his being by himself. One should not degrade the self. Indeed, the person should be the friend of himself. Or he could be the enemy as well. (6.5)

*The Mahābhārata contains no chapter headings. This title was assigned by the translator on the basis of verse 12 of this chapter.

The personal energies are the friend of the person by whom those energies are subdued. But for one whose personality is not self-possessed, the personal energies operate in hostility like an enemy. (6.6)

The directive part of a self-controlled, peaceful person remains composed in the cold, heat, pleasure, pain, and also in honor and dishonor. (6.7)

The yogi who is satisfied with knowledge and realized experience, who is stable and who has conquered his sensual energy, who regards a lump of clay, a stone or gold in the same way, is said to be disciplined in yoga. (6.8)

A person who is indifferent to friend, acquaintance, and enemy, who is evenly-disposed to enemies and kinsmen, who exhibits balanced judgment towards saintly people or sinful ones, is to be regarded with distinction. (6.9)

In isolation, the yogi should constantly concentrate on the self. Being alone, he should be of controlled thinking and subdued self without desire and without possessions. (6.10)

In a clean place, fixing for himself a firm seat which is not too high, not too low, with a covering layer of cloth, antelope skin and kusha grass underneath, (6.11)

...being there, seated in a posture, having the mind focused, the person who controls his thinking and sensual energy, should practise the yoga discipline for self-purification. (6.12)

Holding the body, head and neck in balance, steady without movement, gaze at the tip of the nose, not looking in any other direction. (6.13)

With a pacified self, free from fears, with a vow of sexual restraint firmly practised, with mind controlled and having Me in his thought with his mind concentrated, he should sit, being devoted to Me as the Supreme Objective. (6.14)

Disciplining himself continuously as described, the yogi who has a subdued mind, experiences spiritual security. He achieves the extinction of mundane affinity as he simultaneously attains the highest living state. He achieves an existential position with Me. (6.15)

But Arjuna, yoga practice does not consist of eating too much. And it is not the practice of not eating at all, nor the habit of sleeping too much nor staying awake either. (6.16)

For a person who is regulated in eating and in leisure, who is disciplined in the endeavor of duties, who is moderate in sleeping and waking, for him, the yoga practice is a distress-remover. (6.17)

When with tightly controlled thought, he is attentive to his spiritual core self alone, being freed from desires and from all cravings, he is said to be proficient in yoga. (6.18)

This comparison is recalled: A lamp in a windless place which does not flicker, and a yogi of controlled thought who performs disciplines in relation to the spiritual self. (6.19)

At the place where being restrained by yoga practice, thinking stops, and at the place where the yogi perceives the self by the self, he is satisfied in the self. (6.20)

He knows the whereabouts of that continuous happiness, which is grasped by the intellect and which is beyond the mundane senses. And being established, he does not shift from that reality. (6.21)

And having attained that, he thinks there is no greater attainment. Being established in that, he is not drawn away, even by deep distress. (6.22)

Let it be understood, that this separation from emotional distress is the mastery of yoga. This yoga is to be practised with determination and without depressing thought. (6.23)

Abandoning without exception, all desires which are produced from motivation, and completely restraining the total sensual energy by the mind, (6.24)

...little by little, with a firm grasp by the intelligence, he should withdraw from sensual activity. Having made his mind to be fixed on the spiritual self, he should not think of anything. (6.25)

To wherever the unsteady, drifty mind wanders, from there he should restrain it. He should direct the mind to control it in the self. (6.26)

Indeed, being psychologically pacified, the yogi, whose emotions are calmed, who is on the spiritual plane, who is free from bad tendencies, experiences superior happiness. (6.27)

Applying the yoga disciplines constantly to the self, the yogi being freed from faults, easily contacting the spiritual plane, attains endless happiness. (6.28)

With a spirit existing in every creature, and with every creature based on a spirit, a person who is proficient in yoga, perceives the same existential arrangement in all cases. (6.29)

To him who sees Me in all forms and who sees all creatures in reference to Me, I am never out of range, and he is never out of My view. (6.30)

Although moving in various circumstances, the yogi who is established in that harmony, who honors Me as being existentially situated in all creatures, remains in touch with Me. (6.31)

He who, in reference to himself, sees the same facilities in all cases, regardless of pleasure or painful sensations, he, O Arjuna, is considered as the highest yogi. (6.32)

Arjuna said: O slayer of Madhu, due to a shifty vision, I do not see this standard position of a comparatively similar view which is yielded by this yoga practice, declared by You. (6.33)

Unsteady indeed is my mind, O Krishna. It is troublesome, impulsive and resistant. I think that controlling it is comparable to controlling the wind. It is very difficult to accomplish. (6.34)

The Blessed Lord said: Undoubtedly, O powerful man, the mind is difficult to control. It is unsteady. By practice, however, O son of Kuntī, by indifference to its responses, also, it is restrained. (6.35)

For the undisciplined person, yoga is difficult to master. This is My opinion. For the disciplined one, however, by endeavor, it is possible to acquire the skill by an effective means. (6.36)

Arjuna said: What about the undisciplined person who has faith? Having deviated from yoga practice, having not attained yoga proficiency, what course does he take, O Krishna? (6.37)

Is he not like a faded cloud, lost from both situations, like being without a foundation? O Almighty Krishna: He is baffled on the path of spirituality. (6.38)

You can, O Krishna, remove this doubt of mine fully. Besides You, no other remover of doubt, exists here. (6.39)

The Blessed Lord said: O son of Pṛthā, it is realized that neither here on earth nor above in the celestial regions, does the unaccomplished yogi lose his skill. Indeed, O dear Arjuna, no performer of virtuous acts, goes down permanently into misfortune. (6.40)

After obtaining the celestial places where the virtuous souls go, having lived there for many, many years, the fallen yogi is born into the social circumstances of the purified and prosperous people. (6.41)

Alternately, he is born into a family of enlightened people. But such a birth is very difficult to attain in this world. (6.42)

In that environment, he is inspired with the cumulative intellectual interest from a previous birth. And from that time, he strives again for yoga perfection, O dear son of the Kurus. (6.43)

Indeed, by previous practice, he is motivated, even without conscious desire. He who persistently inquires of yoga, instinctively sees beyond the Veda, the spoken description of the spiritual reality. (6.44)

From a steady effort and a consistently controlled mind, the yogi who is thoroughly cleansed of bad tendencies, who is perfected in many births, reaches the supreme goal. (6.45)

The yogi is superior to other types of ascetics; he is also considered to be superior to the masters of philosophical theory, and the yogi is better than the ritual performers. Hence, be a yogi, Arjuna. (6.46)

Of all yogis, the one who is attracted to Me with his soul, who worships Me with full faith, is regarded as being most devoted to Me. (6.47)

CHAPTER 7

Krishna:

The Ultimate Reality*

The Blessed Lord said: With attention absorbed in Me, O son of Pṛthā, practicing yoga, being dependent on Me, you will know of Me fully without a doubt. Hear of this. (7.1)

I will explain the information and give the experience to you without deleting anything. Having known that, no other experience would be left to be discovered in this world. (7.2)

Someone, in thousands of human beings, strives for psychological perfection. Of those who endeavor, even of those who are perfected, someone knows Me in truth. (7.3)

Solid substance, liquid substance, flame, gas, space, mindal energy, intelligence, and initiative are My apportioned, eight-sectioned mundane energy. (7.4)

That is inferior. But, O strong man, know of My other higher energy which consists of the hosts of individual spirits, through which this universe is sustained. (7.5)

---

*The Mahābhārata contains no chapter headings. This title was assigned by the translator on the basis of verse 7 of this chapter.

This higher energy functions as the multiple origins of all creatures. Understand this. I am the cause of production as well as destruction of the entire universe. (7.6)

O conqueror of rich countries, no other reality is higher than Myself. All this existence relies on Me, like pearls strung on a string. (7.7)

I am represented as taste in water, O son of Kuntī . I am signified as light in the moon and sun, as the sacred syllable Om in all the Vedas, as the sound in the atmosphere, as the manliness in men. (7.8)

I am represented as wholesome odor in the earth. I am sensed by the brilliance in the sun, by the life in all creatures. I am indicated by the austerity of the ascetics. (7.9)

Know me as the primeval, primary cause of all creatures, O son of Pṛthā. I can be inferred as the intelligence of the geniuses and glimpsed by the splendor of the splendorous things. (7.10)

I am indicated as the strength of the strong, which is free from selfish desire and passionate urges. I am supportive of romance which is not opposed to the Vedic rules of morality, O powerful son of the Bharata family. (7.11)

Regarding the states of being, which are perceptive clarity, enthusiasm, and depression, know that they are produced by Me. But I am not based in them. They are dependent on Me. (7.12)

All this world is stupefied by the three states of being, which are produced by the mundane influence. The world does not recognize Me, Who is higher than these energies and Who is unaffected. (7.13)

Indeed this quality controlled illusion of Mine is supernatural and difficult to transcend. Only those who rely on Me, can see beyond this bewitching energy. (7.14)

The confused evildoers, the lowest of human beings, those whose discrimination is erased by misconceptions, do not take shelter of Me. They are attached to a corrupted existence. (7.15)

Four kinds of good people worship Me, O Arjuna: the distressed one, the inquisitive one, the needy one, and the informed one, O bullish man of the Bharata family. (7.16)

Of these, the informed man who is constantly disciplined in yoga, being singularly devoted, is distinguished indeed. I am fond of this person and he is fond of Me. (7.17)

All these are exalted people. But the informed one is considered to be my personal representative. Indeed, he who is disciplined in yoga practice, is situated with Me as the Supreme Objective. (7.18)

At the end of many births, the informed devotee surrenders to Me, thinking that the son of Vasudeva is essential to everything. Such a great soul is hard to locate. (7.19)

Persons whose experience was overshadowed by contrary desires, plead with other supernatural rulers, following this or that religious procedure, being restricted by their own material nature. (7.20)

I grant unwavering faith to anyone, who with belief, wants to worship any worshipable deity form. (7.21)

Being endowed with this confidence, he thinks of worshipfully petitioning the deity and gets from that source, his desires, as those fulfillments are permitted by Me. (7.22)

But for those with little intelligence, the result is short-lived. The worshippers of the supernatural rulers go to those gods. Those who worship Me, surely go to Me. (7.23)

Though I am beyond their sensual range, the unintelligent think of Me as being limited to their gross perception. They do not realize My higher existence which is imperishable and supermost. (7.24)

I am not visible to everyone, because I am shielded by My yogicly, self-controlled mystic powers. This stupefied population does not recognize Me as not being subjected to shocks of birth and not being liable to existential pressures of change. (7.25)

I know the departed souls and the living creatures, O Arjuna, as well as those beings who are to be born. But no one recognizes Me. (7.26)

O man of the Bharata family, at the beginning of any creation, all beings are influenced by delusion through the urge of liking or disliking and by the delusive influence of the two-fold sensuality. So it is, O scorcher of the enemy. (7.27)

But those people whose sinful propensities are terminated, whose actions are righteous, who are free from the two-fold delusion, who are maintaining firm vows of austerity, do worship Me. (7.28)

Those who, being dependent on Me, strive for permanent release from bodily deterioration and death, know this spiritual existence completely, as well as the Supreme Spirit and the value of cultural activity. (7.29)

Those who know Me as the Lord of mundane beings, Lord of the supernatural rulers and powers, and Supreme Master of religious disciplines, and who know Me even at the time of the final departure from the body, are the ones who know Me with concentrated mental focus. (7.30)

CHAPTER 8

Another Invisible

Existence*

Arjuna said: What is this spiritual reality? What is the Supreme Soul? What is cultural activity, O Supermost Personality? Concerning the sum total gross reality, how is that described authoritatively? And speaking of the Supreme Supernatural Person and Power, what is that described to be? (8.1)

Who is the Supreme Regulator of religious ceremonies and disciplines? How is He located here in this body, O killer of Madhu? And how, at the time of departure from the body, are You to be known by those persons who are subdued? (8.2)

The Blessed Lord said: The spiritual reality is unaffected and supreme. The Supreme Soul is described as a personal existence Who causes the production of the mundane world. Cultural action is known as creative power. (8.3)

*The Mahābhārata contains no chapter headings. This title was assigned by the translator on the basis of the verse above

The sum total gross reality is ever-changing nature. The master of the world is the Lord of the supernatural rulers and powers. O best of the embodied souls, I, Who exist here in the body, am the Supreme Regulator of religious ceremonies and disciplines. (8.4)

If at the end of one's life, one recalls Me in particular, as one gives up the body, one is elevated to My condition of existence. There is no doubt about this. (8.5)

Moreover, whatever texture of existence is recalled when a person abandons his body in the end, to that same type of life, he is projected, O son of Kuntī, always being transformed into that status of life. (8.6)

Therefore, at all times, remember Me and fight. Anchor your mind and intelligence on Me. You will be with Me without doubt. (8.7)

With a mind that does not venture outwards, which is disciplined by yoga practice, a person goes to the divine Supreme Person, while deeply meditating, O son of Pṛthā. (8.8)

He who meditates on the Person Who knows everything, the most ancient of people, the Supreme Supervisor, the most minute factor, the one with unimaginable form, with a radiant body, free of grossness, (8.9)

...and that meditator who even at the time of death, with an unwavering mind, being connected devotedly, with psychological power developed through yoga practice, and having caused the energizing breath to enter between the eyebrows with precision, goes to the Divine Supreme Person. (8.10)

I will briefly explain the process to you, which the knowers of the Veda describe as imperishable, which the ascetics who are free from cravings enter and who desiring to be transferred there, they follow a life of celibacy. (8.11)

Controlling all openings of the body, and restricting the mind in the core of consciousness, situating the energizing energy of the soul in the brain, remaining fixed in yoga concentration, (8.12)

...uttering Om, the one-syllable sound which represents the spiritual reality, meditating on Me, the yogi who passes on, renouncing the body, attains the highest objective. (8.13)

He whose mind does not go to another focus at any time, who thinks of Me constantly, for that yogi who is constantly disciplined in yoga, I am easy to reach, O son of Pṛthā. (8.14)

Approaching me in this way, those great souls who went to supreme perfection are not subjected to rebirth in this shifty, miserable location. (8.15)

Up to Brahmā's world, the populations are subjected to repeated births and deaths, O Arjuna. But in approaching Me, rebirth is not experienced, O son of Kuntī. (8.16)

Those who know the day of Brahmā, which has a limit of one thousand time cycles, and the night of Brahmā, which ends in a thousand time cycles, are the people who know day and night. (8.17)

When the day of Creator Brahmā begins, all this visible world is produced from the invisible world. When his night comes, the manifested energies are reverted back into the invisible world. (8.18)

O son of Pṛthā, this multitude of beings which is repeatedly manifested, is naturally shifted out of visibility at the arrival of each of Brahmā's nights. It again comes into existence at the onset of Brahmā's day. (8.19)

But higher than this, there is another invisible existence, which is higher than the primeval unmanifested states of this dissolvable creation. When all these creatures are disintegrated, that is not affected. (8.20)

That invisible world is unalterable, so it is declared. The authorities say that it is the supreme objective. Attaining that, they do not return here. That place is My supreme residence. (8.21)

That Supreme Person, O son of Pṛthā, is attainable through a devotional relationship and not by any other means. Within His influence, all beings exist. By Him, all the universe is energized. (8.22)

O bullish man of the Bharata family, I will tell you of the departure for the yogis who do or do not return. (8.23)

The summer season, the bright atmosphere, the daytime, the bright moonlight, the six months when the sun appears to move north; if at that time, they depart the body, those people who know the spiritual dimension, go to the spiritual location. (8.24)

The smoky, misty or hazy season, as well as in the night-time, the dark-moon time, the six months when the sun appears to move south; if the yogi departs at that time, he attains moonlight, after which he is born again. (8.25)

The light and the dark times are two paths which are considered to be perpetually available for the universe. It is considered so by the authorities. By one, a person goes away not to return; by the other he comes back again. (8.26)

Knowing these two paths, O son of Pṛthā, the yogi is not confused at all. Therefore at all times, be disciplined in yoga practice, O Arjuna. (8.27)

The yogi, having known all this, goes beyond the good results which are derived from study of the Veda, beyond religious ceremonies and disciplines, beyond austerities and beyond offering scripturally-recommended gifts in charity. He goes to the Supreme Primal State. (8.28)

CHAPTER 9

The Devotional Attitude*

The Blessed Lord said: But I will explain to you who are not cynical, the most secret truths, the knowledge with the experience, which having known, you will be freed from impurities. (9.1)

This is the ultimate information, the greatest secret, the purifier of consciousness. It is plain to see, righteous, easy to practise and thoroughly consistent. (9.2)

People who have no faith in this righteous behavior, who have not attained Me, are born again in the cyclic course of death and rebirth, O stern subduer of the enemy. (9.3)

This world is pervaded by My invisible form. All beings survive on My energy but I am not surviving on theirs. (9.4)

And the created beings are not existing on Me. Behold My psychological supremacy. While sustaining the beings and not existing on them, I Myself cause them to be. (9.5)

As the powerful wind is always situated in space and is pervasive, so all beings exist under My influence. Consider this thoroughly. (9.6)

*The Mahābhārata contains no chapter headings. This title was assigned by the translator on the basis of verse 26 of this chapter.

O son of Kuntī, all beings retrogress into My own material nature at the end of Brahmā's day. I produce them again at the beginning of Brahmā's next day. (9.7)

On the foundation of material nature, I repeatedly produce this whole multitude of beings, which is powerless in respect to the potency of material nature. (9.8)

And these cultural activities do not bind Me, O conqueror of rich countries. Since I am situated indifferently, I remain unattached to the activities. (9.9)

With Me as the supervisor, material nature produces moving and nonmoving things. By this cause, O son of Kuntī , the universe operates. (9.10)

The foolish people, not knowing My higher existence as the Almighty God of the beings, hold a low opinion of Me as having a human body. (9.11)

Persons with vain hopes, purposeless actions, and incorrect information, who lack discrimination, being wicked and devilish, rely on the deluding feature of material nature. (9.12)

But great souls, being reliant on the supernatural level of material nature, worship Me, without deviation, knowing Me as the originator of beings, the constant factor. (9.13)

Always glorifying Me, endeavoring with firm vows, paying respect to Me with devotion, being always disciplined, they worship Me. (9.14)

By the discipline of concepts, others do perform regulated worship of Me as the Singular Basis and as the Variety, facing all levels of reality simultaneously. (9.15)

I am represented as the Vedic ritual. I may also be seen as the sacrificial ceremony or as the sanctified offering. I may be regarded as the medicinal herb. I may be seen as the ghee, fire or oblation given. (9.16)

I am the father of this universe, the mother, the creator, the grandfather, the subject of education, the purifier, the sacred syllable Om, the Rig, Sama, and Yajur Vedas. (9.17)

I am the objective, the supporter, the master, the observer, the existential residence, the shelter, the friend, the origin, the cause of universal integration, the foundation, the reservoir of energies, and the non-deteriorating cause. (9.18)

I produce heat. I withhold and release rainfall. I arrange the relatively-long life span of celestial bodies and the quick death of the earthly ones, as well as the short-term existence and eternal life. (9.19)

The knowers of the three Vedas, the soma drinkers, and those who are reformed of bad tendencies, worship Me with sacrificial procedures. They desire to be transferred to heaven. Attaining the merit-based world of Surendra, the king of the angelic people, they enjoy celestial delights in the astral region. (9.20)

Having enjoyed the multi-dimensional, angelic paradise world, exhausting their pious merits, they enter the world of short-life duration. Thus adhering to the tri-part Vedic injunctions for righteous life style, those who aspire for pleasures and luxuries get the opportunity to go to heaven and come back to the earth again. (9.21)

I tend to the welfare of the persons who worship no other person but Me, who keep their minds attuned to Me, and who always cultivate the yoga disciplines. (9.22)

Those who, with religious ceremonies, disciplines and faith, devotedly worship other supernatural rulers, indirectly petition Me, O son of Kuntī, although they do not perform the ceremonies and disciplines by My recommendation. (9.23)

Indeed I am the Master of all religious ceremonies and disciplines and I am the person Who should appreciate such procedures. But they do not recognize Me; hence they deviate from the path of virtue. (9.24)

Those who satisfy the supernatural rulers, go to those authorities. Those who satisfy the pious ancestors, associate with such departed spirits. Those who try to satisfy the ghosts, go to those beings. Those who try to satisfy Me, surely approach Me. (9.25)

I do accept that given devotion from a disciplined, purified person who offers Me a leaf, flower, fruit or water with a devotional attitude. (9.26)

Whatever you do, whatever you eat, whatever you present ceremonially, whatever you give away, whatever you perform as a discipline, O son of Kuntī, do that as an offering to Me. (9.27)

Thus you will be liberated from good and bad consequences and from the implications that come from action. Being liberated by the discipline of yoga as it was applied to renunciation, you will come to Me. (9.28)

I am equally disposed to all beings. No one is shunned by Me nor is anyone especially dear to Me. But those who worship Me with devotion are My favorite and I am special to them too. (9.29)

If a wicked person worships Me without being devoted to any other authority, he is considered saintly, for he decided correctly. (9.30)

He quickly becomes a person whose character is virtuous. He experiences the eternal spiritual peace. O son of Kuntī , take note of it! No devotee of Mine is ruined permanently. (9.31)

O son of Pṛthā, by relying on Me, even persons from sinful parentage, even women, businessmen, even laborers, do move towards the supreme goal. (9.32)

How much more accessible then, is it for the piously-inclined brahmins and yogi kings? Having acquired an opportunity in this temporary, miserable world, you should devote yourself to Me. (9.33)

With the mind fixed on Me, being devoted to me, performing ceremonial worship to Me, make obeisance to Me. Being thus disciplined, with Me as the Supreme Objective, you will come to Me. (9.34)

CHAPTER 10

A Fraction of Krishna's Splendor*

The Blessed Lord said: Again, O powerful man, hear from Me of the supreme information. Desiring your welfare, I will explain it, O beloved one. (10.1)

The supernatural rulers do not know My origin, nor do the great yogi sages. In all respects, I am the source of the supernatural rulers and the great yogi sages. (10.2)

Of those who use perishable bodies, the one who regards Me as birthless and beginningless and who knows that I am the Almighty God of the world, is the perceptive person. He is freed from all faults. (10.3)

Intelligence, knowledge, sanity, patience, truthfulness, self-control, tranquility, pleasure, pain, existence, non-existence, fear, fearlessness... (10.4)

...non-violence, impartiality, contentment, austerity, charity, fame and infamy, are multiple existential conditions, which are derived from Me alone. (10.5)

*The Mahābhārata contains no chapter headings. This title was assigned by the translator on the basis of verse 41 of this chapter.

The seven great yogi sages of old, the four celibate boys, and also the primal sexually-disciplined procreators come from Me, being produced mentally. From them, the creatures of this universe evolved. (10.6)

Whosoever experiences in reality, this divine glory and extensive mystic discipline of Mine, becomes harmonized with Me by consistent yoga practice. There is no doubt about this. (10.7)

I am the originator of all. From Me, everything proceeds. Thinking of Me in this way, the intelligent persons, who are endowed with meditative ability, worship Me. (10.8)

Those who think of Me, who concentrate the life energy on Me, who enlighten one another and speak of Me constantly, are content and happy. (10.9)

Of those who are constantly disciplined, who worship with affection, I give the technique by which they draw near to Me. (10.10)

In the interest of assisting them, I, who am situated within their beings, cause the ignorance produced by the stupefying influence of material nature to be banished by their clear realized insight. (10.11)

Arjuna said: Hail to You Who are the Supreme Reality, the Supreme Refuge, the Supreme Reformer, O Lord. You are the eternal divine Person, the Primal God Who is birthless, and Whose influence spreads everywhere. (10.12)

All the yogi sages, as well as the supernatural yogi sage Narada, Asita Devala, and Vyasa declare this of You. And You Yourself state this to me. (10.13)

All that You say to me is true. I believe it, O Kesava. Indeed it is not possible to understand You, O Bhagavan, Blessed Lord. Neither the supernatural rulers nor their enemies, the descendants of Danu, can know Your form. (10.14)

You alone know Yourself, O Supreme Person, O maintainer of the creatures, O Lord of the created beings, O God of gods, O Lord of the universe. (10.15)

Please describe, thoroughly, Your supernatural wondrous manifestations by which You pervade these worlds and are situated in them. (10.16)

How will I know You, Mystic Master, O Yogi? Is it by constantly meditating? In what aspects of existence are You to be considered by Me, O Blessed Lord? (10.17)

Explain in more detail about Your self-disciplinary methods and the resultant mystic power and of Your splendorous form, O motivator of the people. There is no final satisfaction for me in hearing Your sweet words. (10.18)

The Blessed Lord said: Listen, I will talk to you of the most prominent of my supernatural manifestations, O best of the Kuru clan, for there is no limit to My influence. (10.19)

O sleep regulator, I am the person Who is situated in the mystic resting place of all beings. I am responsible for the beginning, middle, and end of all beings. (10.20)

Of the Ādityas, I am Vishnu. Of lights, I am represented by the radiant sun. Of the thunderstorms, I am represented by Marīci. Of the stars, I am signified by the moon. (10.21)

Of the Vedas, I am represented by the Sāma Veda. Of the supernatural rulers, I am represented as Vāsava Indra. Of the senses, I am represented as the mind. In creature forms, I am represented as consciousness. (10.22)

Of the cosmic destroyers, I am represented by the Shankara Shiva. Of the Yakshas and Rakshas, I am best represented as Vittesha Kubera. Of the Vasus, I am represented by Pāvaka Agni. Of the mountains, I am represented as Mount Meru. (10.23)

O son of Pṛthā, know Me as being represented by Brihaspati, the chief of the family priests. Of military commanders, I am represented by Skanda. Of the seas, I am symbolized by the ocean. (10.24)

Of the great yogi sages, Bhrigu is one whom I am best represented by. Of the spoken words, I am represented by the one-syllable sound. Of the religiously-motivated disciplines, I am represented best by the discipline of uttering prayers. Of stationary objects, I am best represented by the Himalayas. (10.25)

Of all trees, I am best represented by the Ashvattha sacred fig tree. Of the supernatural yogi sages, I am represented by Narada. Of the supernatural singers, it is Chitraratha; of the perfected souls, the yogi philosopher Kapila. (10.26)

Of horses, know Me as represented by the supernatural horse Uccaihśrava, which was born of the sweet celestial sea. Of the kingly elephants, know Me as represented by Airāvata, and know Me as the King of men. (10.27)

Of weapons, I am compared to the Vajra supernatural thunderbolt. Of cows, I am represented as the supernatural Kamadhuk. And in the case of begetting, I am represented by Kandarpa, the god of romance. Of serpents, I am represented by Vāsuki. (10.28)

I am represented by Ananta among the supernatural snakes. I am represented by Varuṇa, among the aquatics. Among the piously-departed spirits, I am represented by Aryamā. Of the subduers, I am represented by Yama. (10.29)

And I am represented as Prahlāda among the titan descendants of Diti, as time of the monitors, as the king of beasts among the animals, as the son of Vinata among the birds. (10.30)

Among the cleansers, I am best represented by the wind. Of the weapon carriers, I am best represented by Rāma. Of the sea monsters, I am represented by the shark. Of the rivers, I am represented by Jahnu's daughter. (10.31)

Of creations, I am represented by the formation, continuation and ending. O Arjuna, of the sciences, I am knowledge of the Supreme Soul. I am represented by the conclusion of the logicians. (10.32)

Of letters, I am represented by the letter A. Of the word combinations, I am represented by the two-word compound. I am comparable to infinite time. I am represented by Dhātā, the four-faced Brahmā. (10.33)

I am represented as all-devouring death. I am the foundation of things that are to be produced. And among women, I am represented by Kīrti, the goddess of fame, Śrī, the goddess of fortune, Vāk, the goddess of speech, Smṛti, the goddess of recollection, Medhā, the goddess of counsel, Dhṛti, the goddess of faithfulness and Kṣama, the goddess of patience. (10.34)

Of the Sāma Veda chants, the Brihat Sāma melody represents Me. Of the poetic hymns, I am the Gayatri. Of months, I am best represented by the November-December lunar month. Of the seasons, I am best compared to Spring. (10.35)

I am represented as the gambling skill of the swindlers. I am compared to the splendor of the splendid things. I am compared to victory and endeavor. I am the reality of the realistic things. (10.36)

Of the Vṛṣṇis, I am the son of Vasudeva. Of the Pāṇḍavas, I am represented by Arjuna. Of the yogi philosophers, I am compared to Vyāsa. Of the poets, I am represented by the respected poet Uśanā. (10.37)

Of rulers, I am the authority to punish. For those seeking victory, I may be compared to the means of morality; of secrets, I am represented by silence. In wise men, I am represented as knowledge. (10.38)

And O Arjuna, I am the origin of all created beings. There is nothing active or stationary which could exist without My influence. (10.39)

There is no end to My supernatural manifestations, O burner of the enemy forces. This was explained by Me as a sampling of My extensive opulence. (10.40)

You should realize that whatever fantastic existence, whatever prosperous or powerful object there is, in any case, it originates from a fraction of My splendor. (10.41)

But Arjuna, what is the value of this extensive information? As the foundation, I support this entire universe with a fraction of Myself. (10.42)

CHAPTER 11

The Universal Form*

Arjuna said: As a matter of mercy to me, the highest, most private information of the Supreme Soul was explained by You in this lecture. Subsequently, the delusion departed from me. (11.1)

The description of origin and ruination of the beings was heard in detail by me, O Person Whose eyes are shaped like lotus petals. You also described Your eternal majestic glory. (11.2)

This is as You explained about Yourself, O Supreme Lord. I wish to see Your Majestic Form, O Supreme Person. (11.3)

If You think that it is possible for me to see this, O Lord, Master of the yoga technique, then make me see You in that Eternal Form. (11.4)

The Blessed Lord said: O son of Pṛthā, see My forms in the hundreds or rather in the thousands, variously manifested, supernatural and of the various colors and shapes. (11.5)

Look at the supernatural rulers, the supernatural destroyers, the two supernatural doctors and the supernatural stormers. View many wonders which were unseen before, O relation of the Bharata family. (11.6)

*The Mahābhārata contains no chapter headings. This title was assigned by the translator on the basis of verse 16 of this chapter.

Here, O conqueror of sleep, you see the entire universe with all active and inactive manifestations, situated as one reality, in My body. And observe any other manifestations which you desire to see. (11.7)

But you cannot see with your vision. I give you supernatural sight to look at My mystic majesty. (11.8)

Sanjaya said: O King, having said that, the great Master of yoga, Hari, the God Vishnu, revealed to the son of Pṛthā, the Supreme Form, the supernatural glory. (11.9)

Countless mouths, eyes, wondrous visions, countless supernatural ornaments, supernatural uplifted weapons, (11.10)

...wearing supernatural garlands and garments, with supernatural perfumes and ointments, appearing all wonderful, the God appeared infinite as He faced all directions. (11.11)

Imagine in the sky, a thousand suns, being at once risen together. If such a brilliance were to be, it might be compared to that Great Personality. (11.12)

There the entire universe existed as one reality divided in many ways. Arjuna Pandava then saw the God of gods in that body. (11.13)

Then he, who was amazed, whose hair bristled, Arjuna, the conqueror of rich countries, bowing his head to the God, with palm pressed for prayers, spoke. (11.14)

Arjuna said: I see the supernatural rulers in Your body, O God, as well as all varieties of beings assembled there, Lord Brahmā, who is lotus-seated, all the yogi sages and the supernatural serpents. (11.15)

There are countless arms, bellies, faces, and eyes. I see You in all directions, O person of infinite form. There is no end, no middle, nor even a beginning of You. I observe You, O Lord of all, O Form of everything. (11.16)

This Form is crowned, armed with a club, bearing a discus, a mass of splendor on all sides, shining wondrously with immeasurable radiance of the sun and blazing fire. I see You in entirety, You Who are difficult to behold. (11.17)

You are the indestructible Supreme Reality, to be realized. You are the ultimate shelter of all. You are the imperishable, eternal guardian of law. It seems to me that You are the most ancient person. (11.18)

You who are without beginning, middle, or ending, Who has infinite manly power, Who has unlimited arms, Who has the sun and moon as Your eyes, I see You, with the blazing oblation-eating mouth, heating this universe with Your Own splendor. (11.19)

In all directions, the space between heaven and earth is pervaded by You alone. Seeing Your marvelous Form, of a terrible feature, the three worlds tremble, O great Personality. (11.20)

Those groups of supernatural rulers enter You. Some being terrified, bowing with palms pressed together, offer praise. "May everything be suitable," they say. The groups of great yogi sages and perfected yogis praise You with lavish glorification. (11.21)

The supernatural destroyers, the supernatural rulers, the assistants to those rulers, these and the Sādhya guardian angels, the Vishvadeva supernatural priests, the two primal supernatural doctors, the supernatural stormers, the spirits who take vapor bodies, the groups of celestial musicians, the spirits guarding natural resources, the supernatural rebels and the perfected souls, behold You. And they are all amazed. (11.22)

O mighty-armed Person, having seen Your great Form with many mouths, and many arms, thighs, and feet, many bellies and many terrible teeth, the worlds tremble as well as I. (11.23)

Having seen You, sky extending, blazing, multi-colored, with gaping mouths and blazing vast eyes, there is a shivering in my soul. I find no courage, nor stability, O God Vishnu . (11.24)

And seeing Your Form with many mouths, having terrible teeth, glowing like the fire of universal destruction, I cannot determine the cardinal points. I do not find any peace of mind. Have mercy, O Lord of the gods, Abode of the universe. (11.25)

And those, all the sons of Dhṛtarāṣṭra, along with the groups of rulers, Bhishma, Droṇa, as well as that son of the charioteer, along with our men and also our chief warriors, are in contrast to You. (11.26)

They speedily enter Your fearful mouths, which have dreadful teeth. Some cling between the teeth. They are seen with crushed heads. (11.27)

As the water currents of many rivers flow to the sea, so the earthly heroes enter Your mouths, which are flaming. (11.28)

As moths speedily enter a blazing fire to destruction, so to ruination, the worlds enter Your mouths with great speed. (11.29)

You lick, swallowing from all sides, all the worlds with Your flaming mouths, filling the universes with splendor, Your horrible blazing rays burn it, O Lord Vishnu . (11.30)

Explain to me who You are, O respected Person of terrible form. I gave my homage to You, O best of gods. Have mercy! I want to understand You, O Primal Person. I do not know Your intentions. (11.31)

The Blessed Lord said: I am the time limit, the mighty world-destroying Cause, appearing here to annihilate the worlds. Even without you, all the armored warriors, in both armies will cease to live. (11.32)

Therefore you should stand up! Get the glory! Having conquered the enemies, enjoy a prosperous country. These fellows are supernaturally disposed by Me already. Be only the agent, O ambidextrous archer. (11.33)

Droṇa, Bhishma, Jayadratha, and Karṇa, as well as other battle heroes, were supernaturally hurt by Me. You may physically kill them. Do not hesitate. Fight! You will conquer the enemies in battle. (11.34)

Sanjaya said: Having heard the speech of the handsome-haired Krishna, Arjuna, the crowned one, who was trembling, offered respect with joined palms. Bowing again, he stutteringly, with much fright and prostrations, spoke to Krishna. (11.35)

Arjuna said: Everything is in position, O Hṛṣīkeśa, masterful controller of the senses. The universe rejoices and is delighted by Your fame. The demons being terrified, flee in all directions. All the groups of perfected souls will reverentially bow to You. (11.36)

And why should they not bow to You, O great soul, original creator, Who is also greater than Brahmā, Who is the infinite Lord of the gods, the resort of the world? You are the imperishable basis of energies, the sum total permanent life, the sum total temporary existence, and whatever is beyond all that. (11.37)

You are the First God, the most ancient spirit. You are the knower, You are the supreme refuge of all the worlds. You are that which is to be known. You are the ultimate sanctuary. By You, the universe is pervaded, O Person of Infinite Form. (11.38)

You are represented by Vāyu, the wind regulator; Yama, the death supervisor; Agni, the fire controller; Varuṇa, the master of the waters; Śāśaṅka, the moon Lord; Procreator Brahmā; and you are the father of Brahmā. Obeisances unto You a thousand times repeatedly. Again and again, honor to You! (11.39)

Reverence to You from the front, from behind. Let there be obeisances to You on all sides, O sum total Reality. You are infinite power, immeasurable might. You penetrate everything. In that sense, You are Everything. (11.40)

Whatever was said impulsively, considering You as a friend, such as, "Hey, Krishna! Hey, family man of the Yadus! Hey, buddy!" was done by me through ignorance of Your majestic supernatural glory or even by affectionate familiarity. (11.41)

And with intent to joke, You were disrespectfully treated, while playing, while on a couch, while sitting, while dining privately or even in public, O infallible Krishna. For that I ask forgiveness of You Who are boundless. (11.42)

You are the father of the world, of the moving and non-moving objects. You are the worshipable and gravest spiritual master. There is none like You in the three partitions of the universe. How could anyone be greater, O person of incomparable splendor? (11.43)

Therefore, bowing with reverence, lying my body down, I ask for mercy of You, O Lord Who is to be praised. As a father to a son, as a friend to his chum, as a beloved to a lover, You should be merciful, O God. (11.44)

Seeing what was never seen before, I am delighted but my mind trembles with fear. Now, O God, cause me to see the God-form. Have mercy, O Lord of the gods, shelter of the world. (11.45)

I wish to see You wearing a crown, armed with a club, and with a disc in hand, as requested. Please become that four-armed form, O thousand-armed Person, O Person of universal dimensions. (11.46)

The Blessed Lord said: By My grace to you Arjuna, this Supreme Form was manifested from My yoga power. This Form of Mine which is made of supernatural energy, being universal, infinite and primal, was never seen by another other person besides you. (11.47)

Not by Vedic sacrificial ceremonies, nor by Vedic education, not by offering charity as recommended in the Vedic literatures and not by special ritual acts, nor by strenuous austerities, can I be seen in such a form in this world of human beings except through the method used by you, O great hero of the Kurus. (11.48)

You should not tremble nor be confused after seeing this, My ghastly form. Be free from fear and be cheerful of mind. Again look at this form of Mine. (11.49)

Sanjaya said: Krishna, the son of Vasudeva, having said this to Arjuna, revealed His own Divine Form. And once again that great person assumed the pleasing, attractive form and caused the frightened Arjuna to be calm. (11.50)

Arjuna said: Seeing this gentle, human-like Form of Yours, O Janardana, motivator of human beings, I am satisfied with my mind returned to the normal condition. (11.51)

The Blessed Lord said: This Form of Mine which you saw, is difficult to perceive. Even the supernatural rulers always wish for the sight of this Form. (11.52)

Neither by Vedic study, nor by austerity, nor by charity, and not by sacrificial ceremony, can I be seen in the way you saw Me. (11.53)

By undistracted devotion only, O Arjuna, can I be
known, seen in reality, and communicated with,
O scorcher of enemies. (11.54)

Whosoever does My work, depending on Me,
being devoted to Me, abandoning attachment,
being freed from hostility towards all beings,
comes to Me, O son of Pṛthā. (11.55)

CHAPTER 12

The Most Disciplined Yogi*

Arjuna said: Of those who are constantly disciplined in yoga, being also devoted to You, and those who cherish the imperishable invisible existence, which of these two have the highest knowledge of the yoga techniques? (12.1)

The Blessed Lord said: Those whose minds are focused on Me, who are always disciplined in yoga, who are always involved in worship of Me, who are endowed with the highest degree of faith, they are considered to be the most disciplined. (12.2)

But those who cherish the imperishable, undefinable, invisible, all-pervading, inconceivable, unchanging, immovable, constant reality, (12.3)

...by controlling all sensual energies, being even-minded in all respects, rejoicing in the welfare of all creatures, they also attain Me. (12.4)

The mental exertion of those whose minds are attached to the invisible existence is greater. The goal of reaching that invisible reality is attained with difficulty by the human beings. (12.5)

*The Mahābhārata contains no chapter headings. This title was assigned by the translator on the basis of verse 2 of this chapter.

But those who defer all actions to Me, regarding Me as the most important factor, who meditate on Me with undistracted yoga discipline, do worship Me. (12.6)

I am the deliverer of those devotees, rescuing them from the vast existence of death and reincarnation. O son of Pṛthā, I soon deliver those devotees whose thoughts are intently invested in Me. (12.7)

Placing your mind on Me alone, causing your intellect to be absorbed in Me alone, you will be focused on Me from now onward. There is no doubt about this. (12.8)

If, however, you cannot steadily anchor your thoughts on Me, then by yoga practice, try to attain Me, O conqueror of wealthy countries. (12.9)

But if perchance, you are incapable of such practice, then by being absorbed in My work, or even by doing activities for My sake, you will attain perfection. (12.10)

If you are unable to even do this, then resorting to My yoga process, abandoning all results of action, act with self restraint. (12.11)

Indeed, derived knowledge is better than practice. Meditation is superior to derived knowledge. Renunciation of results is better than meditation. From such renunciation, spiritual peace is instantly gained. (12.12)

One who does not dislike any of the creatures, who is friendly and compassionate, free from attachment to possessions, free from the propensity of "I am the creator of my actions," being equally disposed towards pain and pleasure, being patient, (12.13)

...the yogi who is always content, who has a controlled self, who is determined, whose mind and intellect are focused on Me, who is devoted to Me, is dear to Me. (12.14)

He from whom the world is not repulsed, and who is not repulsed from the world, who is free from excitement, impatience, fear and distress, is dear to Me. (12.15)

He who is impartial, hygienic, competent, indifferent, whose anxieties are gone, who abandoned all personal undertakings, and who is devoted to Me, is dear to Me. (12.16)

One who does not rejoice, nor hate, nor lament, nor crave, who left aside what is agreeable and disagreeable, who is full of devotion, is dear to Me. (12.17)

Being equally disposed to an enemy and a friend, with a similar attitude in honor and dishonor, in cold and heat, happiness and distress, being free from attachment, (12.18)

...one who relates equally to condemnation and glorification, who is silent, content with anything, who is unattached to home, who has a steady mind, and who is full of devotion, that person is dear to Me. (12.19)

Those who honor these life-giving codes of behavior, who have confidence, being intent on Me as top-priority, being devoted, are very dear. (12.20)

CHAPTER 13

Material Nature

The Person

The Living Space*

Arjuna said: What is material nature? What is the person? What is the living space? Who is the experiencer of the living space? I wish to know this. What is a conclusion? And what is experienced, O Keshava, pretty-haired One? (13.1)

The Blessed Lord said: This, the earthly body, O son of Kuntī, is called the living space. Those who are knowledgeable of this, declare the person who understands this to be the experiencer of the living space. (13.2)

Know also, that I am the experiencer of all living spaces, O man of the Bharata family. Information of the living space and the experiencer of it, is considered by Me to be knowledge. (13.3)

As for this living space, as for what is, as for what kind of environment it is, as for the changes it endures, as to what causes it to change, as for he who is involved, as for his potential, hear from Me of that in brief. (13.4)

*The Mahābhārata contains no chapter headings. This title was assigned by the translator on the basis of verse 1 of this chapter.

This was distinctly recited many times with the various Vedic hymns and with the Brahma Sūtras, conclusively with sound logic, by the great yogi sages. (13.5)

The major categories of the elements, the personal initiative, the intellect, the unmanifested energy, the ten and one senses, the five attractive objects, (13.6)

...desire, hatred, pleasure, pain, the whole body, consciousness and conviction; this is described with brevity, as the living space with its changes. (13.7)

Lack of pride, freedom from deceit, non-violence, patience, straightforwardness, attendance to a teacher, purity, stability and self-restraint, (13.8)

..indifference towards the attractive objects, absence of motivated initiative, the perception of the danger of birth, death, old age, disease, and suffering, (13.9)

...social and emotional detachment towards child, wife, a home and whatever is related to social life, being always even-minded towards what is desired and what is not wanted, (13.10)

...unswerving devotion to Me, with no other discipline but yoga practice, resorting to a secluded place, having a dislike for crowds of human beings, (13.11)

...constantly considering information about the Supreme Spirit, perceiving the value of the science of reality; this is declared as knowledge. Whatever is contrary to this, is ignorance. (13.12)

I will explain that which is to be experienced, knowing which one gets in touch with eternal life. The beginningless Supreme Reality is said to be neither substantial nor insubstantial. (13.13)

Everywhere is Its hands and feet, everywhere Its eyes, head and face, everywhere is Its hearing ability in this world; It stands, ranging over all. (13.14)

It has the appearance of having all sensual moods, and It is freed from sensuousness. Though unattached, It maintains everything. Though free from the influence of material nature, It is the experiencer of that influence nevertheless. (13.15)

It is outside and inside the moving and non-moving beings. Because of Its subtlety, this beginningless Supreme Reality is not comprehended. This Reality is situated far away and it is in the location as well. (13.16)

It is undivided among the beings, but It appears as if It is divided in each. It is the sustainer of the beings and this should be known. It is the absorber and producer. (13.17)

This is declared as the light of the luminaries, but It is beyond gross or subtle darkness. It is the information, the education and the goal of education. It is situated in the psychological core of all beings. (13.18)

Thus the psychological environment as well as the standard knowledge and what is to be known, was described in brief. Experiencing this, My devotee draws near to My state of being. (13.19)

Know that both material nature and the spiritual personality are beginningless, and know that the changes of the living space and the moods of material nature are produced from material nature. (13.20)

Material nature is said to be the cause in terms of created work, sensual potency and agency. The spiritual personality is said to be the cause in terms of experiencing pleasure and pain. (13.21)

The spirit, being situated in material nature, experiences the modes which were produced by that nature. Attachment to the modes is the cause of the spirit's emergence from realistic and unrealistic situations. (13.22)

The observer, the permitter, the supporter, the experiencer, the Supreme Lord and the Supreme Soul as He is called, He is the highest spirit in the body. (13.23)

He who knows the spiritual person and material nature, along with the variations of material nature, is not born again, regardless of his present condition. (13.24)

Some perceive the spirit by the spirit through meditative perception of the spirit. Others do so with Sāṁkhya philosophical conclusions and others by yogic disciplined action. (13.25)

But some, though they are ignorant, hear from others. They worship and by their confidence in what is heard, they also transcend death. (13.26)

As for anything that is produced in this existence, be it a stationary or moving object, know, O strong man of the Bharatas, that it is produced from a synthesis of the experiencer and the living space. (13.27)

The Supreme Lord is similarly situated in all beings without perishing when they disintegrate. He who perceives that, really sees. (13.28)

Seeing the same Lord being situated everywhere, he does not degrade the soul by his own soul. Subsequently, he goes to the supreme destination. (13.29)

He who sees, that in all cases, the actions are performed by material nature, and who regards himself as a non-doer, truly sees. (13.30)

When a person sees that all the various states of being are based on a single foundation, and only from that everything emanates, then he reaches the spiritual plane. (13.31)

Since this imperishable Supreme Lord is beginningless and devoid of the influence of material nature, even though He is situated in the material body, O son of Kuntī, He does not act or become contaminated. (13.32)

As by subtlety, the all-pervading space is not polluted, so the soul, though situated all over the body, is not affected actually. (13.33)

As the sun alone illuminates the whole world, O man of the Bharata family, so the user of the living space gives feeling to the entire psyche. (13.34)

Those who by intuitive perception know the difference between the living space and the experiencer, as well as the liberation of the living being from material nature, go to the Supreme. (13.35)

CHAPTER 14

The Extensive Mundane

Reality*

The Blessed Lord said: I will explain more, giving the highest information of all knowledges, the very best. Having experienced that, all the yogi philosophers went away from here to the Supreme Perfection. (14.1)

Resorting to this experience, being transformed into a nature that is similar to My own, they are not born even at the time of the universal creation, nor are they disturbed at the time of dissolution. (14.2)

The extensive mundane reality is My womb. I impregnate the essence into it. The origin of all beings comes from that reality, O man of the Bharata family. (14.3)

Forms are produced in all types of wombs, O son of Kuntī, I am the seed-giving father. The extensive mundane reality is the great womb. (14.4)

Clarity, impulsion and retardation are the influences produced of material nature. They captivate the imperishable embodied soul in the body, O strong-armed hero. (14.5)

*The Mahābhārata contains no chapter headings. This title was assigned by the translator on the basis of verse 3 of this chapter.

Regarding these influences, the clarifying one is relatively free from perceptive impurities. It is illuminating and free from disease, but by granting an attachment to happiness and to expertise, it captivates a person, O sinless one. (14.6)

Know that the impulsive influence is characterized by passion. It is produced from earnest desire and attachment. O son of Kuntī, this mode captivates the embodied soul by an attachment to activity. (14.7)

But know that the depressing mode is produced of insensibility which is the confusion of all embodied beings. This captivates by inattentiveness, laziness and sleep, O man of the Bharata family. (14.8)

The clarifying influence causes attachment to happiness. The impulsive one causes a need for action, O Bharata family man. But the depressing mode obscures experience and causes attachment to negligence. (14.9)

When predominating over impulsiveness and depression, clarity emerges, O Bharata family man. Depression rises, predominating over impulsiveness and clarity. Similarly, impulsion takes control over depression and clarity. (14.10)

When clear perception, true knowledge, is felt in all openings of the body, then it should be concluded that the clarifying mode is predominant. (14.11)

Greed, overexertion, rash undertakings, restlessness and craving, these are produced when impulsiveness is predominant, O strong man of the Bharatas. (14.12)

Lack of clarity, lack of energy, inattentiveness and confusion emerge when depression is predominant, O dear son of the Kurus. (14.13)

When the embodied soul goes through the death experience while under the dominance of the clarifying mode, he is transferred to the pure world of those who know the Supreme. (14.14)

Having gone through the death experience in the impulsive mode, the soul is born among the work-prone people; likewise when dying in the depressive mode, the soul takes birth from the wombs of the ignorant species. (14.15)

The authorities say that the result of a well-performed action is in the clarifying mode and is free of defects. But the result of an impulsive act is distress, while the consequence of a depressive act is ignorance. (14.16)

Factual knowledge is produced from clarity. Greed comes from impulsion. Inattentiveness, confusion, and ignorance come from depression. (14.17)

Those who are anchored in clarity, go upward. Those who are impulsive are situated in the middle. Those who are habituated to the lowest influence of the material energy, the retarded people, go downward. (14.18)

When the observer perceives no performer besides the influences of material nature and knows what is higher than those influences, he reaches My level of existence. (14.19)

When the embodied soul transcends these three influences of material nature which are formulated in the body, he is released from birth, death, old age, and distress, and attains immortality. (14.20)

Arjuna said: In regards to a person who transcended the three influences of material nature, by what features is he recognized, O respectful Lord? What is his conduct? And how does he transcend the three influences? (14.21)

The Blessed Lord said: O son of Pandu, he does not scorn nor does he yearn for the presence or absence of enlightenment, enthusiasm or depression. (14.22)

Being situated in the body, but being detached, not being affected by the influences of material nature, considering that the modes are operating naturally, he who is spiritually-situated, who does not become excited, (14.23)

...to whom pain and pleasure are equally regarded, who is self-situated, to whom a lump of clay, a stone or gold, are regarded in the same way, by whom a loved one and a despised person are treated equally, who is steady of mind, to whom condemnation and congratulations are regarded equally, (14.24)

...who is equally disposed to honor and dishonor, who is impartial to friend or foe, who has renounced all undertakings, is said to have transcended the mundane influences. (14.25)

And a person who serves Me with unwavering, yogicly-disciplined affection and who transcends these mundane influences, is suited for absorption in spiritual existence. (14.26)

...for I am the basis of the immortal, imperishable spiritual existence and of the perpetual rules of social conduct and of absolute happiness. (14.27)

CHAPTER 15

Two Types of Spirits*

The Blessed Lord said: The yogi sages say that there is an imperishable Ashvattha tree which has a root going upwards and a trunk downwards, the leaves of which are the Vedic hymns. He who knows this is a knower of the Vedas. (15.1)

Branches spread from it, upwards and downwards. It is nourished by the mundane influences and the attractive objects are its sprouts. The roots are spread below, promoting action in the world of human beings. (15.2)

Its form is not perceived in this dimension, nor its end, nor beginning nor foundation. With the strong ax of non-attachment, cut down this Ashvattha tree with its well-developed roots. (15.3)

Then that place is to be sought, to which having gone, the spirits do not return to this world again. One should think: I take shelter with that Primal Person, from Whom the creation emerged in primeval times. (15.4)

*The Mahābhārata contains no chapter headings. This title was assigned by the translator on the basis of verse 15 of this chapter.

Those who are devoid of pride and confusion, who have conquered the faults of attachment, who constantly stay with the Supreme Spirit, whose cravings have ceased, who are freed from the dualities known as pleasure and pain, these undeluded souls go to that imperishable place. (15.5)

The sun does not illuminate that place, nor the moon, nor the fire. Having gone to that location, they never return. That is My supreme residence. (15.6)

My partner is in this world of individualized conditioned beings. He is an eternal individual soul but he draws to himself the mundane senses of which the mind is the sixth detection device. (15.7)

Regardless of whichever body that master acquires, or whichever one he departs from, he goes taking these senses along, just as the wind goes with the perfumes from their source. (15.8)

While governing the sense of hearing, the vision, the sense of touch, the sense of taste, the sense of smell and the mind, My partner becomes addicted to the attractive objects. (15.9)

The idiots do not perceive how the spirit departs or remains or exploits under the influence of material nature. But those who have the vision of reality do perceive this. (15.10)

The endeavoring yogis see the spirit as being situated in itself; but even with exertion, the imperfected souls, the thoughtless ones, do not perceive it. (15.11)

That sun-yielding splendor which illuminates the universe completely, which is in the moon and which is in fire; know that splendor to be Mine. (15.12)

And penetrating the earth, I support all beings with potency. And having influenced the sap-producing moon, I cause all plants to thrive. (15.13)

Becoming the Vaiśvānara digestive heat, I, entering the body of all breathing beings and combining with the inhaled and exhaled breath, digest the four kinds of foodstuffs. (15.14)

And I entered the central psyche of all beings. From Me comes memory, knowledge and reasoning. By all the Vedas, I am to be known. I am the author of Vedānta and the knower of the Vedas. (15.15)

These two types of spirits are in this world, namely the affected ones and the unaffected ones. All mundane creatures are affected. The stable soul is said to be unaffected. (15.16)

But the highest spirit is in another category. He is called the Supreme Spirit, Who having entered the three worlds as the eternal Lord, supports it. (15.17)

Since I am beyond the affected spirits and I am even higher than the unaffected ones, I am known in the world and in the Vedas as the Supreme Person. (15.18)

In this way, he who is undeluded, who knows Me as the Supreme Person, he being knowledgeable, worships Me with all his being, O man of the Bharata family. (15.19)

Thus the most secret teaching is declared by Me, O blameless man. Having realized this, O descendant of the Bharatas, one becomes a wise person, whose duties are accomplished. (15.20)

CHAPTER 16

Two Types of Created Beings*

The Blessed Lord said: Fearlessness, purity of being, consistency in application of yoga to mental concepts, charity, self-restraint, worship ceremony, recitation of scripture, austerity and straight-forwardness, (16.1)

...non-violence, recognition of reality, absence of anger, abandonment of consequences, spiritual security, absence of destructive criticism, compassion for the beings, freedom from craving, gentleness, modesty, absence of fickleness, (16.2)

...vigor, forbearance, strong-mindedness, purity, freedom from hatred, and the freedom from conceit; these are the talents of those born with the godly nature, O descendant of Bharata. (16.3)

Deceit, arrogance, conceit, anger, abusive language, and lack of knowledge are the tendencies of those born with a wicked nature, O son of Pṛthā. (16.4)

*The Mahābhārata contains no chapter headings. This title was assigned by the translator on the basis of verse 6 of this chapter.

The godly talent is conducive to liberation. It is considered that the wicked tendencies facilitate bondage. Do not worry. You are endowed with the godly nature, O son of Pandu. (16.5)

There are two types of created beings in this world, the godly type and the wicked. The godly type was explained in detail. Hear from me of the wicked, O son of Pṛthā. (16.6)

The wicked people do not know what to do and what not to do. Neither cleanliness or even good conduct, nor realism is found in them. (16.7)

They say that the universe is unreal, without a foundation, without a Supreme Lord, without a series of causes. They explain, saying, "Sexual urge is the cause. What other basis could there be?" (16.8)

Holding this view, men who lost track of their spirituality, who have negligible intelligence, who commit cruel acts, become enemies for the destruction of the world. (16.9)

Being reliant on the non-fulfilling lusty urge, possessed of hypocrisy, pride, and intoxication, having accepted unrealistic views, through delusion, they proceed with impure objectives. (16.10)

And clinging to endless worries which end at the time of death, with lusty enjoyment as the highest aim, being convinced that this is all there is, (16.11)

...bound by hundreds of frustrating expectations, cherishing craving and anger, using any means, they strive to acquire huge sums of money for the fulfillment of craving and pleasure. (16.12)

Thinking: "This was obtained by me today, I will fulfill this fantasy. This is it. This wealth will also be mine. (16.13)

"That enemy was killed by me, I will kill others as well. I am the controller. I am the enjoyer. I am successful, powerful and happy. (16.14)

"I am rich and upper class. Who is there besides me? I will perform religious ceremony. I will donate. I will make merry." This is what is said by those who are deluded by ignorance. (16.15)

Being carried away by many ideas, being occupied by entangling delusions, being attached by cravings and enjoyments, they fall into an unclean, hellish condition. (16.16)

Self-conceited, stubborn, possessed of pride and the arrogance of having money, with hypocrisy and without reference to Vedic injunctions, they worship in ceremonies that are religious in name only. (16.17)

Clinging to a misplaced self-identity, brute force, arrogance, craving and anger, those who are envious dislike Me, in their own bodies and in those of others. (16.18)

I constantly hurl the despising cruel, vicious, lowest of humans into the cycles of rebirth in the wombs of wicked people. (16.19)

Thus, O son of Kuntī, entering the wombs of the wicked people, the blockheads, after not associating with Me in birth after birth, traverse the lowest route of transmigration. (16.20)

Craving, anger and greed are the three avenues of hell which degrade the soul. Therefore one should abandon this threefold influence. (16.21)

Being released from these three avenues of depression, O son of Kuntī , a person serves his best interest and then goes to the highest destination. (16.22)

Whosoever discards the scriptural injunctions, and follows the impulsive inclinations, does not get perfection or happiness or the supreme destination. (16.23)

Therefore, setting your standard of duty and non-duty by scriptural recommendation, knowing the scriptural rules prescribed, you should perform actions in this world. (16.24)

CHAPTER 17

Three Types of

Confidences*

Arjuna said: Concerning those who disregard scriptural injunction, but who with full confidence perform religiously-motivated ceremonies and austerities, what indeed, is their position, O Krishna? Is it clarity, impulsion or depression? (17.1)

The Blessed Lord said: According to innate tendency, there are three types of confidences of the embodied souls. These are clarifying, motivating and depressing. Hear about this. (17.2)

Confidence becomes manifest according to the essential nature of the person, O man of the Bharata family. A human being follows his trend of confidence. Whatever type of faith he has, that he expresses only. (17.3)

The clear-minded people worship the supernatural rulers. The impulsive ones worship the passionate sorcerors and the cannibalistic humans. The others, the retarded people, petition the departed spirits and the hordes of ghosts. (17.4)

*The Mahābhārata contains no chapter headings. This title was assigned by the translator on the basis of verse 2 of this chapter.

People who endure terrible austerities which are not recommended in the scripture, people who are enthused with deceit and misplaced identity, who are possessed with craving, rage and brute force, (17.5)

...those who torture the collection of the elements which comprise the body, who also trouble Me within the body, know that they have wicked intentions. (17.6)

But food as well, which is liked by all, is of three kinds as are religious ceremony, austerity and charity. Hear of the difference between them. (17.7)

Foods which increase the duration of the life, the spiritual well-being, strength, health, happiness and satisfaction, which are juicy, milky, sustaining and palatable, are eatables which are dear to the clear-minded people. (17.8)

Foods which are pungent, sour, salty, peppery, acidic, dry and overheated, are desired by the passionate people. These foods cause pain, misery and sickness. (17.9)

Food which is stale, tasteless, and rotten, which was left over, as well as that which is rejected or unfit for religious ceremony, is cherished by the depressed people. (17.10)

A religious discipline or ceremony in observance of the scripture, by those who do not desire a benefit and who, while concentrating, think, "This is to be sacrificed," is a ceremony of the realistic type. (17.11)

But when a benefit is kept in mind and when the motive is to outsmart the deity, know, O best of the Bharatas, that the disciplinary worship offered is based on impulsion. (17.12)

When scripture is neglected, food is not offered, Vedic hymns not recited, a fee not given to the priest, and confidence is lacking, regard that disciplinary worship as depressive. (17.13)

Reverential respect of the supernatural rulers, of those who are qualified by the sacred thread ceremony, of the spiritual teacher, and of the wise man, purity, straightforwardness, celibacy and non-violence, are said to be austerity of the body. (17.14)

Speech which does not cause distress, and is truthful, agreeable and beneficial, as well as regular recitation of the scriptures is the discipline of speech. (17.15)

Peace of mind, gentleness, silence, self restraint, and purity of being, this is called discipline of mind. (17.16)

When this threefold austerity is performed with the highest faith by yogicly-disciplined people who do not aspire for a benefit, the authorities consider it to be realistic. (17.17)

Austerity which, in this world is performed with trickery for the sake of reputation, respect and reverence, is declared to be impulsive, shifty and temporary. (17.18)

Austerity performed with foolish, mistaken ideas, and with torture or for the purpose of harming someone else, is said to be depressive. (17.19)

A gift given to one who has not done a prior favor, in the proper place and time and to a worthy person, is remembered as being virtuous. (17.20)

But the gift which is given grudgingly for a compensation or alternately hoping for a reward, is mentally noted as being impulsive. (17.21)

That gift which is given in the wrong place and time, to an unworthy person, without paying respect, without due consideration, is said to be of the depressive mode. (17.22)

The pronouncement Om Tat Sat is known as the threefold designation of spiritual reality. By this expression, the brahmins, the Vedas, and the prescribed religious disciplines and ceremonies were ordained in ancient times. (17.23)

Hence as prescribed in the Vedic scriptures, acts of sacrifice, charity, and austerity always begin by the spiritual masters while uttering the sound Om. (17.24)

While saying Tat without an interest in a benefit, acts of sacrifice, austerity and various types of charity are performed by those who are desirous of liberation. (17.25)

The word Sat is used to mean reality and excellence and also for a praiseworthy act, O son of Pṛthā. (17.26)

Steady application in sacrifice, austerity and charity, is also called Sat. An action which is supportive of this purpose is also designated as Sat. (17.27)

An oblation offered with a lack of faith and austerity performed in the same way is called asat, unrealistic, O son of Pṛtha. And that has no value to us here or in the hereafter. (17.28)

CHAPTER 18

The Most Secret of All

Information*

Arjuna said: Regarding the rejection of opportunity, O strong-armed hero, I want to know the fact. And regarding the rejection of consequences, O Hṛṣīkeśa, distinguish these, O slayer of Keshi. (18.1)

The Blessed Lord said: The authoritative speakers know the rejection of opportunity as renunciation of actions which are prompted by craving. The clear-sighted seers declare the abandonment of the results of benefit-motivated action as the rejection of consequences. (18.2)

Some philosophers declare that action is to be abandoned, since it is full of faults. Some others say that acts of sacrifice, charity and austerity are not to be abandoned. (18.3)

Hear my view on this matter of abandonment of the consequences of action, O best of the Bharatas. The abandonment of consequences, O tiger among men, is designated as being threefold. (18.4)

*The Mahābhārata contains no chapter headings. This title was assigned by the translator on the basis of verse 64 of this chapter.

Acts of sacrifice, charity, and austerity are not to be abandoned but should be performed. Sacrifice, charity and austerity are purificatory acts even for the wise men. (18.5)

But these actions are to be performed by giving up attachment to results, O son of Pṛthā. This is definitely My highest opinion. (18.6)

But renunciation of obligatory actions is not proper. The rejection of it on the basis of delusion, is said to occur by the influence of depression. (18.7)

He who abandons action because of difficulty or because of a fear of bodily suffering, performs impulsive renunciation. He would not obtain the desired result of that renunciation. (18.8)

O Arjuna, when an action is done in a disciplinary manner, because it is to be performed, and with renunciation of the attachment to the results, it is considered to be in the clarifying mode. (18.9)

The renouncer who is filled with clarity, the wise man whose doubts are removed, does not hate disagreeable action, nor is he attached to agreeable performance. (18.10)

Indeed it is not possible for the body-supported beings to abandon actions completely. But whosoever is the renouncer of the results of actions is called a renunciate. (18.11)

Undesired, desired and mixed are the three types of results of actions that occur for the departing souls who do not renounce results. But for the renouncers of opportunity, there is no result at all. (18.12)

Learn from Me, O mighty-armed man, of the five factors declared in the Sāṁkhya doctrine for the accomplishment of all actions. (18.13)

The location, the agent, the various instruments, the various movements, and destiny, the fifth factor. (18.14)

As for whatever project a human being undertakes with body, speech and mind, regardless of it being moral or immoral, these are its five factors. (18.15)

In that case, whosoever regards himself as the only agent, does not perceive correctly. This is due to the defective intellect of the idiot. (18.16)

Regarding the person whose attitude is not falsely assertive, whose intellect is not clouded, even after slaying these people, he would not have slain or have been implicated. (18.17)

Experience, the item of research, and the experiencer are the three aspects which serve as the impetus for action. The instruction, the action itself, and the agent are three parts of an action. (18.18)

In the Sāṁkhya analysis of the influence of material nature, it is stated that experience, action, and the agent are of three types as categorized by the influence of material nature. Hear correctly of these as well. (18.19)

That experience by which one perceives one imperishable being in all beings, undivided in the divided, know it to be an experience in clarity. (18.20)

But that experience by which one realizes different beings of different kinds with differences in all beings, should be known as experience in the impulsive mode. (18.21)

But that experience which appears to be the whole vision, being attached to one procedure without due cause, without a valid purpose, being petty, that is said to be of the depressive influence. (18.22)

Action which is controlled, which is free from attachment, which is performed without craving or repulsion, without desire for results, such action is said to be of the clarifying influence. (18.23)

But that action which is performed with a wish for cravings, with false assertion or alternately with much effort, that is said to be of the impulsive influence. (18.24)

That action which is undertaken from a misconception, regardless of the consequence, the damage and the violence, and without considering one's practical power, is said to be of the depressive mode. (18.25)

A performer who is free from attachment, free from vanity, who is consistent and perseverant, and who is unaffected in success or failure, is rated to be in the clarifying mode. (18.26)

A performer who is prone to impulsiveness, who craves the results of action, who is greedy, violent by nature, unclean and who is prone to joy or sorrow, is declared to be under the impulsive mode. (18.27)

A performer who is undisciplined, vulgar, stubborn, wicked, deceitful, lazy, depressed and neglectful, is said to be in the depressive mode. (18.28)

Now, O conqueror of wealthy countries, hear of the three types of intellect and also of determination, explained thoroughly and distinctly, according to their distinctions under the influences of material nature. (18.29)

That intellectual insight which discerns when to endeavor and when not to strive, what should be done and what should not be done, what is dangerous and what is safe, what brings restrictions and what gives freedom, that O son of Pṛthā, is in the clarifying mode. (18.30)

That intellectual insight by which right and wrong, duty and neglect are mistakenly identified, is, O son of Pṛthā, in the impulsive mode. (18.31)

That intellectual insight which is absorbed by ignorance, which considers the wrong method as the right one and perceives all values in a perverted way, is O son of Pṛthā, of the depressive mode. (18.32)

The determination which holds the mind, the energizing breath, and the senses by constant yoga expertise, that, O son of Pṛthā, is of the clarifying influence. (18.33)

But the determination by which one holds duty, pleasure, and wealth with attachment and with desire for results, is an impulsion, O son of Pṛthā. (18.34)

That determination by which an idiot does not abandon sleep, fear, sorrow, despair and pride, is of the depressing mode. (18.35)

But now hear from Me, O strong man of the Bharatas, regarding the three types of happiness which one either enjoys from habit or through which one comes to the end of sorrow. (18.36)

That which initially is like poison but which changes into an experience like nectar and which is felt through the clarity of spiritual discernment is said to be happiness in the clarifying mode. (18.37)

That happiness which in the beginning seems like nectar and which comes from the contact between the sense organs and attractive objects, which changes as if it were poison, is recognized as an impulsion. (18.38)

And that happiness which in the beginning and in consequence is bewildering to the person, which comes from sleep, laziness and confusion, is said to be of the depressive mode. (18.39)

There is no object on earth nor even in the subtle mundane domains, that can exist without these three modes which were produced from material nature. (18.40)

The activities of the priestly teachers, the ruling sector, the productive managers and the working class, are allotted by the modes of material nature which arise from natural tendencies. (18.41)

Tranquility, restraint, austerity, cleanliness, patience, straightforwardness, knowledge, discrimination and a belief in God, are the work of a priestly teacher based on his natural tendencies. (18.42)

Heroism, majesty, determination, expertise, lack of cowardice in battle, charitable disposition, and governing tendency are the actions of a ruling human being, based on natural tendency. (18.43)

Agriculture, cow-tending and trading are the productive manager's activity based on natural tendency. Service actions are produced of a working class person based on natural tendency. (18.44)

A human being attains perfection by being content in the consistent execution of his duty. Hear of the means through which a duty-satisfied person finds perfection. (18.45)

Through the performance of his own duty, a human being finds perfection by worshipping the Person from Whom the beings originate and by Whom all this is pervaded. (18.46)

Better to attend to one's own duty imperfectly than to heed another's perfectly. By performing actions which are restricted by one's own nature, one does not acquire fault. (18.47)

One should not abandon inborn duty, O son of Kuntī, even if it is faulty. Indeed, all undertakings are with defect, even as fire is shrouded with smoke. (18.48)

He whose intellect is unattached in every application, who is self-controlled, whose yearnings disappeared, by the renunciation of opportunities, attains supreme perfection of being exempt from action. (18.49)

Learn from Me briefly, O son of Kuntī, how a person who attained perfection, also reaches a spirituality which is the highest. (18.50)

Being yogically-disciplined with purified intelligence and controlling the soul, firmly abandoning sound and other attractive sensations, rejecting craving and hatred, (18.51)

...living in isolation, eating lightly, controlling speech, body and mind, always being devoted to yogic meditation, resorting to dispassion, (18.52)

...freeing oneself from a false assertion, from the application of brute force, from arrogance, from craving and from possessiveness, being unselfish and peaceful, one is suited to the spiritual level. (18.53)

One who is absorbed in the spiritual existence, who has a peaceful spirit, who does not lament nor hanker for anything, who is impartial to all beings, attains the supreme devotion to Me. (18.54)

By devotion to Me, he realizes how great I am and who I am in reality. Then having known Me in truth, he enters My association immediately. (18.55)

Furthermore, know that while performing all actions, he whose reliance is always on Me, gets by My grace, the eternal imperishable abode. (18.56)

Renouncing by thought, all actions to Me, being devoted to Me, relying on the process of disciplining the intellect by yoga, be constantly thinking of Me. (18.57)

Thinking of Me, you will, by My grace, surpass all difficulties. But if by false assertion, you do not listen, you will be lost. (18.58)

While relying on a false assertive attitude, you may think, "I will not fight." But that determination is mistaken. Your material nature will force you. (18.59)

By your natural tendencies, being bound by obligations, O son of Kuntī, that which you do not want to perform due to delusion, you will do even if it is against your will. (18.60)

The Lord of all beings is situated in the central psyche, O Arjuna, causing all beings to transmigrate by His mystic power, just as if they were fixed to a spinning machine. (18.61)

With your whole being, go only to Him for shelter, O descendant of Bharata. You will attain the supreme security and the eternal place by His grace. (18.62)

The information that is more secret than secret was explained by Me to you. Having considered this fully, you may act as you please. (18.63)

Hear again of My supreme discourse, the most secret of all information. You are surely loved by Me. Hence I speak for your benefit. (18.64)

Be mindful of Me, be devoted to Me. Sacrifice to Me. Do bow to Me. In this way you will in truth come to Me. I promise for you are dear to Me. (18.65)

Abandoning all traditional conduct, take refuge in Me alone. I will cause you to be free of faults. Do not worry. (18.66)

This should not be told by you to anyone who does not perform austerity or is not devoted at anytime, or does not desire to hear what is said or is critical of Me. (18.67)

Whosoever, having performed the highest devotion to Me, will explain this supreme secret to My devotees, will certainly come to Me. (18.68)

And no one among human beings is more pleasing to Me in performance than he. And no one on earth will be more dear to Me than he, (18.69)

I would be loved by the devotee who by sacrifice of his knowledge, will study this sacred conversation of ours. This is My opinion. (18.70)

Even the person who hears with confidence, without ridiculing is freed. He should attain the happy worlds where persons of pious actions reside. (18.71)

Was this heard by you, O son of Pṛthā, with a one-pointed mind? Was your ignorance and confusion removed, O conqueror of wealthy countries? (18.72)

Arjuna said: Through Your grace, the confusion is removed, memory is retrieved by Me, O unaffected one. I stand clear of doubts. I will execute Your instruction. (18.73)

Sanjaya said: In this way, I heard this talk of the son of Vasudeva and the great-souled son of Pṛthā. It is amazing. It causes the hairs to stand on end. (18.74)

By the grace of Vyasa, I am the one who heard this secret information of the supreme yoga from the Lord of yoga, Krishna, who Himself explained it directly. (18.75)

O King, remembering repeatedly, this amazing and holy talk between Keśava and Arjuna, I rejoice again and again. (18.76)

And remembering repeatedly that super-fantastic form of Hari, my astonishment is great, O King, and I excitedly rejoice again and again. (18.77)

Wherever there exists the Lord of yoga, Krishna, wherever there is the son of Pṛthā, the bowman, there would surely be splendor, victory, prosperity and morality. This is my opinion. (18.78)

OM TAT SAT

END

Index

LIST OF TEACHERS

Gaudiya Vaishnava teacher:

    Srila Bhaktivedanta Swami Prabhupada

Hatha yoga teacher: Swami Vishnudevananda

Kundalini yoga teacher: Yogi Harbhajan Singh

Celibacy yoga teachers: Swami Shivananda,
    Srila Yogiraj Yogeshwarananda

Purity-of-the-psyche yoga teacher:
    Srila Yogiraj Yogeshwarananda

Kriya yoga teachers: Srila Babaji Mahasaya,
    Siddha Swami Muktananda

Brahma yoga teacher:

    Siddha Swami Nityananda

About the Author

Michael Beloved (Madhvāchārya dās) took his current body in 1951 in Guyana. In 1965, while living in Trinidad, he instinctively began doing yoga postures and trying to make sense of the supernatural side of life.

Later on, in 1970, in the Philippines, he approached a Martial Arts Master named Mr. Arthur Beverford, explaining to the teacher that he was seeking a yoga instructor; Mr. Beverford identified himself as an advanced disciple of Sri Rishi Singh Gherwal, an astanga yoga master.

Mr. Beverford taught the traditional Ashtanga Yoga with stress on postures, attentive breathing and brow chakra centering meditation. In 1972, Madhvāchārya entered the Denver Colorado Ashram of Kundalini Yoga Master Sri Harbhajan Singh. There he took instruction in Bhastrika Pranayama and its application to yoga postures. He was supervised mostly by Yogi Bhajan's disciple named Prem Kaur.

In 1979 Madhvāchārya formally entered the disciplic succession of the Brahma-Madhava Gaudiya Sampradaya through Swami Kirtanananda, who was a prominent sannyasi disciple of the Great Vaishnava Authority Sri Swami Bhaktivedanta Prabhupada, the exponent of devotion to Sri Krishna.

After carefully studying and practicing the devotional process introduced by Sri Swami Bhaktivedanta Prabhupada, Madhvacharya was inspired to do a translation of the Bhagavad-Gītā. At the time, his personal Deities were a small marble set of Śrī Śrī Krishna-Balaram Murtis. Lord Balaram encouraged him to take a closer look at what Sri Krishna actually said in the Gītā and to consider its relevance to the history which became known as the Mahābhārata. It was under that energy of Lord Balaram that this translation was produced.

This translation does not concern religious affiliation. It is designed to give readers insight to what Sri Krishna and Arjuna discussed in the discourse, without any effort to convince or convert the reader. It is free of missionary overtones.

Krishna said this about those who study the Bhagavad-Gītā:

adhyeṣyate ca ya imaṁ dharmyaṁ
saṁvādamāvayoḥ

jñānayajñena tenāham iṣṭaḥ syāmiti me matiḥ
(18.70)

I would be loved by the devotee who by sacrifice of his knowledge, will study this sacred conversation of ours. This is My opinion. (18.70)

Publications

English Series

Bhagavad Gita English
Anu Gita English
Markandeya Samasya English
Yoga Sutras English
Uddhava Gita English

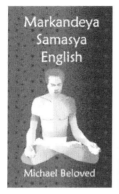

These are in 21st Century English, very precise and exacting. Many Sanskrit words which were considered untranslatable into a Western language are rendered in precise, expressive and modern English, due to the English language becoming the world's universal means of concept conveyance.

Three of these books are instructions from Krishna. **In Bhagavad Gita English** and **Anu Gita English**, the instructions were for Arjuna. In the **Uddhava Gita English,** it was for Uddhava. Bhagavad Gita and Anu Gita are extracted from the Mahabharata.

Uddhava Gita was extracted from the 11th Canto of the Srimad Bhagavatam (Bhagavata Purana). One of these books, the **Markandeya Samasya English** is about Krishna, as described by Yogi Markandeya, who survived the cosmic collapse and reached a divine child in whose transcendental body, the collapsed world was existing. Another of these books, the **Yoga Sutras English,** is the detailed syllabus about yoga practice.

My suggestion is that you read **Bhagavad Gita English**, the **Anu Gita English,** the **Markandeya Samasya English,** the **Yoga Sutras English** and lastly the **Uddhava Gita English**, which is much more complicated and detailed.

For each of these books we have at least one commentary, which is published separately. Thus your particular interest can be researched further in the commentaries.

The smallest of these commentaries and perhaps the simplest is the one for the Anu Gita. We published its commentary as the Anu Gita Explained. The Bhagavad Gita explanations were published in three distinct targeted commentaries. The first is Bhagavad Gita Explained, which sheds lights on how people in the time of Krishna and Arjuna regarded the information and applied it. Bhagavad Gita is an exposition of the application of yoga practice to cultural activities, which is known in the Sanskrit language as karma yoga.

Interestingly, Bhagavad Gita was spoken on a battlefield just before one of the greatest battles in the ancient world. A warrior, Arjuna, lost his wits and had no idea that he could apply his training in yoga to political dealings. Krishna, his charioteer, lectured on the spur of the moment to give Arjuna the skill of using yoga proficiency in cultural dealings including how to deal with corrupt officials on a battlefield.

The second commentary is the <u>Kriya Yoga Bhagavad Gita</u>. This clears the air about Krishna's information on the science of kriya yoga, showing that its techniques are clearly described free of charge to anyone who takes the time to read Bhagavad Gita. Kriya yoga concerns the battlefield which is the psyche of the living being. The internal war and the mental and emotional forces which are hostile to self-realization are dealt with in the kriya yoga practice.

The third commentary is the <u>Brahma Yoga Bhagavad Gita</u>. This shows what Krishna had to say outright and what he hinted about which concerns the brahma yoga practice, a mystic process for those who mastered kriya yoga.

There is one commentary for the **Markandeya Samasya English**. The title of that publication is <u>Krishna Cosmic Body</u>.

There are two commentaries to the Yoga Sutras. One is the <u>Yoga Sutras of Patanjali</u> and the other is the <u>Meditation Expertise</u>. These give detailed explanations of the process of Yoga.

For the Uddhava Gita, we published the <u>Uddhava Gita Explained</u>. This is a large book and requires concentration and study for integration of the information. Of the books which deal with transcendental topics, my opinion is that the discourse between Krishna and Uddhava has the complete information about the realities in existence. This book is the one which removes massive existential ignorance.

Meditation Series

<u>Meditation Pictorial</u>

<u>Meditation Expertise</u>

<u>Core-Self Discovery</u>

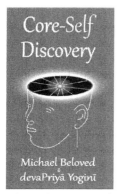

The specialty of these books is the mind diagrams which profusely illustrate what is written. This shows exactly what one has to do mentally to develop and then sustain a meditation practice.

In the **Meditation Pictorial**, one is shown how to develop psychic insight, a feature without which meditation is imagination and visualization, without any mystic experience per se.

In the **Meditation Expertise**, one is shown how to corral one's practice to bring it in line with the classic syllabus of yoga which Patanjali lays out as the ashtanga yoga eight-staged practice.

In **Core-Self Discovery**, one is taken though the course of pratyahar sensual energy withdrawal which is the 5th stage of yoga in the Patanjali ashtanga eight-process complete system of yoga practice. These events lead to the discovery of a core-self which is surrounded by psychic organs in the head of the subtle body. This product has a DVD component for teachers and self-teaching students.

These books are profusely illustrated with mind diagrams showing the components of psychic consciousness and the inner design of the subtle body.

Explained Series

Bhagavad Gita Explained

Uddhava Gita Explained

Anu Gita Explained

The specialty of these books is that they are free of missionary intentions, cult tactics and philosophical distortion. Instead of using these books to add credence to a philosophy, meditation process, belief or plea for followers, I spread the information out so that a reader can look through this literature and freely take or leave anything as desired.

When Krishna stressed himself as God, I stated that. When Krishna laid no claims for supremacy, I showed that. The reader is left to form an independent opinion about the validity of the information and the credibility of Krishna.

There is a difference in the discourse with Arjuna in the Bhagavad Gita and the one with Uddhava in the Uddhava Gita. In fact these two books may appear to contradict each other. In the Bhagavad Gita, Krishna pressured Arjuna to complete social duties. In the Uddhava Gita, Krishna insisted that Uddhava should abandon the same.

The Anu Gita is not as popular as the Bhagavad Gita but it is the conclusion of that text. Anu means what is to follow, what proceeds. In this discourse, an anxious Arjuna request that Krishna should repeat the Bhagavad Gita and again show His supernatural and divine forms.

However Krishna refuses to do so and chastises Arjuna for being a disappointment in forgetting what was revealed. Krishna then cites a celestial yogi, a near-perfected being, who explained the process of transmigration in vivid detail.

Commentaries

Yoga Sutras of Patanjali

Meditation Expertise

Yoga Sutras of Patanjali is the globally acclaimed text book of yoga. This has detailed expositions of yoga techniques. Many kriya techniques are vividly described in the commentary.

Meditation Expertise is an analysis and application of the Yoga Sutras. This book is loaded with illustrations and has detailed explanations of secretive advanced meditation techniques which are called kriyas in the Sanskrit language.

Krishna Cosmic Body is a narrative commentary on the Markandeya Samasya portion of the Aranyaka Parva of the Mahabharata. This is the detailed description of the dissolution of the world, as experienced by the great yogin Markandeya who transcended the cosmic deity, Brahma, and reached Brahma's source who is the divine infant, Krishna.

Anu Gita Explained is a detailed explanation of how we endure many material bodies in the course of transmigrating through various life-forms. This is a discourse between Krishna and Arjuna. Arjuna requested of Krishna a display of the Universal Form and a repeat narration of the Bhagavad Gita but Krishna declined and explained what a siddha perfected being told the Yadu family about the sequence of existences one endures and the systematic flow of those lives at the convenience of material nature.

Bhagavad Gita Explained shows what was said in the Gita without religious overtones and sectarian biases.

Kriya Yoga Bhagavad Gita shows the instructions for those who are doing kriya yoga.

Brahma Yoga Bhagavad Gita shows the instructions for those who are doing brahma yoga.

Uddhava Gita Explained shows the instructions to Uddhava which are more advanced than the ones given to Arjuna.

Bhagavad Gita is an instruction for applying the expertise of yoga in the cultural field. This is why the process taught to Arjuna is called karma yoga which means karma + yoga or cultural activities done with a yogic demcanor.

Uddhava Gita is an instruction for apply the expertise of yoga to attaining spiritual status. This is why it is explains jnana yoga and bhakti yoga in detail. Jnana yoga is using mystic skill for knowing the spiritual part of existence. Bhakti yoga is for developing affectionate relationships with divine beings.

Karma yoga is for negotiating the social concerns in the material world and therefore it is inferior to bhakti yoga which concerns negotiating the social concerns in the spiritual world.

This world has a social environment and the spiritual world has one too.

Right now Uddhava Gita is the most advanced informative spiritual book on the planet. There is nothing anywhere which is superior to it or which goes into so much detail as it. It verified that historically Krishna is the most advanced human being to ever have left literary instructions on this planet. Even Patanjali Yoga Sutras which I translated and gave an application for in my book, Meditation Expertise, does not go as far as the Uddhava Gita.

Some of the information of these two books is identical but while the Yoga Sutras are concerned with the personal spiritual emancipation (kaivalyam) of the individual spirits, the Uddhava Gita explains that and also explains the situations in the spiritual universes.

Bhagavad Gita is from the *Mahabharata* which is the history of the Pandavas. Arjuna, the student of the Gita, is one of the Pandavas brothers. He was in a social hassle and did not know how to apply yoga expertise to solve it. Krishna gave him a crash-course on the battlefield about that.

Uddhava Gita is from the *Srimad Bhagavatam (Bhagavata Purana),* which is a history of the incarnations of Krishna. Uddhava was a relative of Krishna. He was concerned about the situation of the deaths of many of his relatives but Krishna diverted Uddhava's attention to the practice of yoga for the purpose of successfully migrating to the spiritual environment.

Specialty

These books are based on the author's experiences in meditation, yoga practice and participation in spiritual groups:

Spiritual Master
sex you!
Sleep **Paralysis**
Astral Projection
Masturbation Psychic Details

In **Spiritual Master**, Michael draws from experience with gurus or with their senior students. His contact with astral gurus is rated. He walks you through the avenue of gurus showing what you should do and what you should not do, so as to gain proficiency in whatever area of spirituality the guru has proficiency.

sex you! is a masterpiece about the adventures of an individual spirit's passage through the parents' psyches. The conversion of a departed soul into a sexual urge is described. The transit from the afterlife to residency in the emotions of the parents is detailed. This is about sex and you; learn about how much of you comprises the romantic energy of your would-be parents!

Sleep Paralysis clears misconceptions so that one can see what sleep paralysis is and what frightening astral experience occurs while the paralysis is being experienced. This disempowerment has great value in giving you confidence that you can and do exist even if you are unable to operate the physical body. The implication is that one can exist apart from and will survive the loss of the material body.

Astral Projection details experiences Michael had even in childhood, where he assumed incorrectly that everyone was astrally conversant. He discusses the life force psychic mechanism which operates the sleep-wake cycle of the physical form, and which budgets energy into the separated astral form which determines if the individual will have dream recall or no objective awareness during the projections. Astral travel happens on every occasion when the physical body sleeps. What is missing in awareness is the observer status while the astral body is separated.

Masturbation Psychic Details is a surprise presentation which relates what happens on the psychic plane during a masturbation event. This does not tackle moral issues or even addictions but shows the involvement of memory and the sure but hidden subconscious mind which operates many features of the psyche irrespective of the desire or approval of the self-conscious personality.

Online Resources

Visit The Website And Forum

Email:	michaelbelovedbooks@gmail.com
	axisnexus@gmail.com

Website	michaelbeloved.com
Forum:	inselfyoga.com